Penny Pinching Art

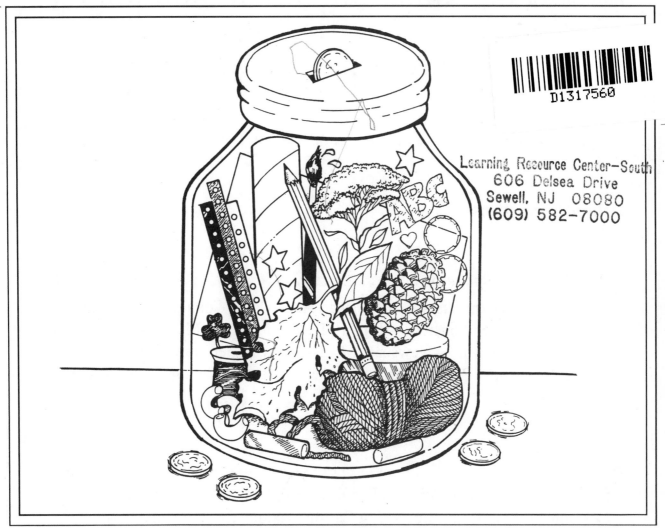

Written by Barbara Lyerly Goins

Edited by Karen Goldfluss

Illustrated by Sue Fullam

Teacher Created Materials, Inc.
P.O. Box 1040
Huntington Beach, CA 92647
©1993 Teacher Created Materials, Inc.
Made in U.S.A.

ISBN 1-55734-139-7

Table of Contents

Table of Contents (cont.)

Introduction

The joy of creating and self-expression through art provides children with a very positive, active involvement in the learning process.

It is important to expose children to classroom experiences in which they are allowed to connect their love of art with purposeful activities in other areas of the curriculum.

Whether you teach thematically, in a whole language environment, or in a traditional classroom setting, art activities can be a vital part of the curriculum.

Most teachers today are faced with the ever-present challenge of the restricted budget, especially when it comes to art supplies. The purpose of this 96 page book, *Penny Pinching Art*, is to provide teachers with art activities that are inexpensive and accessible.

The five sections of art activities in *Penny Pinching Art* include:

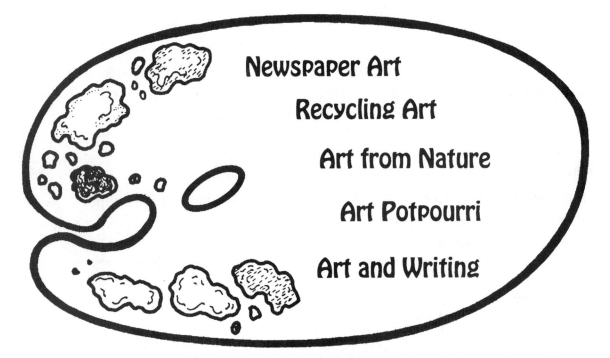

Newspaper Art

Recycling Art

Art from Nature

Art Potpourri

Art and Writing

Each section contains a variety of activities, many of which are multi-purpose. Materials, directions, and suggested activities are listed for each art project.

Teachers are also provided with suggestions for what materials to collect, how to store items to be used for art projects, and a list of easily recycled items from home or community.

We know that with *Penny Pinching Art*, you and your students will come away with many new, inexpensive, and creative ideas for using those materials you may have at one time considered discarding.

Collecting and Storing Materials

Recycle It!

Use any sturdy cardboard containers and boxes with lids to store materials for use throughout the year. The following boxes are easy to obtain and provide a variety of sizes and shapes from which to choose: grocery boxes, shoe boxes, stationery boxes, supply boxes, 10 ream copier paper boxes, and large ice cream containers.

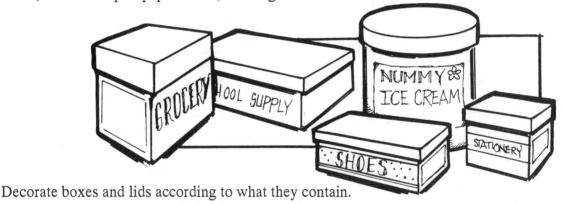

Decorate boxes and lids according to what they contain.

- Use Christmas wrapping paper to decorate boxes that will contain Christmas cards.
- Use newspaper to decorate boxes that will contain old newspapers.
- Decorate a small box with any kind of paper and glue an item or picture on the end to indicate what the box contains. For example, put buttons on a decorated box to indicate that buttons are inside.

Line boxes on shelves so children can easily use them, either to add or take away supplies.

Set boxes on top of lids until the end of the school year; then, use lids to close and store away until needed for another year.

Collecting and Storing Materials *(cont.)*

Box It!

The following items are indispensable in the classroom. Be sure that materials are properly stored in labelled boxes and accessible to both teachers and students.

- newspapers and magazines
- used copier paper
- art tissue
- yarn, ribbon, string, thread, lace
- pipe cleaners
- glitter, sequins, etc.
- buttons
- pine cones, acorns
- corn, beans, and seeds
- lids (plastic)
- paper goods
- juice cans
- sea shells
- cotton swabs and cotton balls
- play money
- old crayons
- paper bags
- fabric bolts
- pretzels
- milk cartons
- plastic produce containers

- scraps of wrapping paper
- construction paper scraps
- cellophane
- pom-poms
- feathers
- old keys
- old or used stamps
- wild flowers
- margarine tubs
- soda pop can tabs
- plastic forks, spoons
- rocks (small)
- toothpicks
- toilet paper/paper towel tubes
- doilies
- left over icicles from Christmas tree
- pizza boards
- craft sticks, wood cubes, etc.
- macaroni
- egg cartons
- stencils

Recycling Made Easy

An excellent way to introduce the idea of saving the environment at the same time you are saving pennies is to begin a classroom recycling center of art materials you will use throughout the year. The following is a list of items and suggestions to help you get started. Give students a sense of purpose and ownership in the project by encouraging them to supply these and other penny pinching materials. Brainstorm ideas for other recycled materials that may be used in the classroom and their possible uses.

Soda Pop Can Tabs

These can be strung together into chains for necklaces, hanging items, etc. Tabs make wonderful additions to collages.

Juice Cans

Cover cans with yarn and glue labels or names on the outside. Decorated cans can be used as gifts or as organizers.

Wood Cubes and Shavings

Use paint or markers to write numbers on cubes and use as dice. Use wood shavings to represent hair on art work, or glue shavings to collages to add texture.

Plastic Forks and Spoons

Make a bouquet or centerpiece of forks, spoons, and dried flowers. Tie them together with ribbon.

Make a stick puppet. With markers, draw a face on a spoon. Add yarn for hair. Glue bits of cloth to the handle to make clothes.

Whatsits

Encourage students to create something new using one item from each classroom recycle box. This is an excellent cooperative group activity.

Rocks

Start a class collection of smooth, round rocks. Make rock creatures by adding eyes, legs, etc., using paint, markers, and recycled materials.

Margarine Tubs

These make excellent storage containers. They can also be used for science projects, planting seeds, water-related experiences, and sorting activities.

Placemats

Collect greeting cards, Christmas cards, etc. Arrange cards on construction paper, glue and let dry. Laminate or use clear contact paper.

Recycling Made Easy *(cont.)*

Paper Bags

Stuff paper bags with newspaper and tie them shut. Decorate bags to make characters from books, plays, etc. (See page 69.) Or, design paper bag puppets (See page 68).

Toothpicks and Cotton Swabs

Use toothpicks to outline or create pictures. Cotton swabs can be glued to paper to make people and scenery. Glue toothpicks together to form toothpick sculptures.

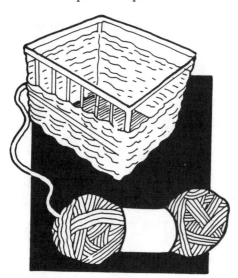

Newspaper Dolls

Crumple newspaper into a ball to form the doll's head. For the body, roll newspaper into shape desired. Roll and bend arms and legs as shown. Tape or tie body parts together. Paint and add features to the doll. Use yarn for hair.

Leaves

Collect an assortment of leaves. Trace on construction paper and draw veins. Or, do crayon rubbing by placing light-weight paper over leaves and rubbing a crayon back and forth across them. Cut out leaf shapes and laminate them for durability.

Plastic Produce Containers

By weaving yarn into the sides of a one-pint (500mL) produce container, students can make decorative gift containers.

Bottle Caps

Make 3-D grape or cherry clusters to use as decorative borders. Draw a pattern for clusters of grapes or cherries. Transfer pattern to heavy paper and cut out. Using felt (green or purple for grapes, red for cherries), draw circles to fit tips of bottle caps. Glue caps, face down, to the heavy paper.

Helpful Suggestions

1. Involve parents in the process and activities.

   - Send letters home listing items you need to collect and recycle. A Supply Request Letter is provided on page 85.
   - Solicit help from moms, dads, and grandparents.
   - Invite family members to help with difficult projects.
   - Send materials home for pre-cutting.
   - Encourage suggestions for related projects.

2. Laminate children's art work.

3. Have samples from each child displayed at Open House. Let children share how they designed and assembled their projects.

4. Avoid the use of glass items, especially with small children.

5. Ask stores for their displays when they are finished.

6. Card companies will sometimes give you left-over cards and envelopes.

7. Obtain round pizza boards from pizza places.

8. Ask for empty fabric bolts from fabric stores.

9. Play classical background music as students work.

10. Read a related story or poem to introduce the activity.

11. Encourage creativity! While patterns are easy to use and attractive, they may limit a child's desire to explore and develop his or her own potential. Art should be fun, adventuresome, and, most of all, an expression of one's self!

12. For variety in texture and appearance, try some of these painting possibilities:

    - Paint by blowing through a straw.
    - Paint on a brown paper bag.
    - Paint on crumpled paper. (Crumple, open up, and paint.)
    - Sprinkle salt on paint.
    - Sprinkle glitter on paint.
    - Paint on corrugated cardboard.
    - Paint on fabric. (You might want to use fabric paint for this.)

A Bounty of Bookmarks

Materials

classified section of the newspaper; scissors; watercolors (Use a commercial product, or prepare the homemade recipe on page 86.); paint brushes; construction or other heavy stock paper scraps; glue; markers (optional)

Directions

1. Cut a rectangle or other oblong shape from construction or heavy stock. Make the bookmark about 3" x 9" (8 cm x 23 cm).

2. Cut out a section from the classified ads of the newspaper. (This section produces the best geometric designs.) It should be smaller than the size of the bookmark. Have students decide what shape or design they would like to make on the bookmark. Students can personalize their bookmarks by cutting out letter shapes to represent their names or initials.

3. Watercolor the cut-out newspaper design. Or, have students outline blocks or color in sections of the newspaper ads with markers. Glue the completed newspaper section on the paper bookmark.

Extensions

- Have students make bookmarks throughout the year. Keep an adequate supply of materials and finished bookmarks in a container so that students can make them at appropriate times during the day. Create both personalized and general bookmarks. These make wonderful gifts and reading incentives.

Peace

Materials

newspaper; pencil; bright-colored butcher paper; scissors; glue; watercolors, crayons, or colored pencils; paint brushes; ruler or large stencil block letters (Letters are provided on pages 92-94.)

Directions

1. Ask students to place one of their hands (with fingers spread) on a piece of newspaper. Use a pencil to outline the hand. Students can help each other with this if necessary. Cut out the hand silhouettes.

2. Draw and cut out letters for PEACE. (Use the newspaper.) You can make free form letters if you wish, or use prepared stencils. The letters will serve as a display title.

3. Color the letters using watercolors, crayons, or colored pencils. Glue letters to the top of a large piece of butcher paper.

4. Glue the cut-out newspaper hands below the PEACE title. Arrange the hands to accommodate the activities you wish to present. (Some suggestions follow.)

Extensions

- Have students write stories, poems, biographical information about famous peacemakers, Nobel Peace Prize winners, ways to spread peace throughout the world, etc. Glue these on butcher pages, arranging the students' writing around their hand silhouettes.

Heart Art

Materials

newspaper; glue; scissors; two different colors of construction paper (one 9" x 12"/23 cm x 30 cm piece and one with smaller dimensions) per project

Directions

1. Cut an 8" x 10" (20 cm x 25 cm) section of newspaper.

2. Have students fold the newspaper sheet in half two or three times. You can fold along the length or width, or a combination of both.

3. Have students cut heart shapes along the folds to produce a variety of hearts on the newspaper. Unfold the sheet of newspaper.

4. Glue the smaller piece of construction paper on top of the larger one.

5. Glue the newspaper hearts sheet on the construction paper background.

   Note: If the fold-and-cut method is too difficult for some students, have them draw and color hearts directly on the sheet of newspaper. Then, glue the sheet to the construction paper.

Extensions

- Have students use the heart art to make Valentine's Day card covers for writing journals and/or "Special Moments" diaries.

- Heart art also serves as a decorative background for bulletin boards displaying students' work.

Color Collages

Materials

two different colored sheets of construction paper, one 8" (20 cm) square and one 7" (18 cm) square for each student; one 6" (15 cm) square from newspaper ad section for each student; scissors; glue; watercolors; paint brushes

Directions

1. Have students watercolor here and there on the square of newspaper, leaving some places white. Encourage the use of a variety of colors. Allow the newspaper to dry.

2. Cut out construction paper and newspaper squares.

3. Glue the newspaper square on the 7" square of construction paper. Glue the 7" square of construction paper on the 8" piece.

Extensions

- Display the students' color collages on a wall using a mosaic pattern. To present a more striking mosaic pattern, use a variety of construction paper squares.

- Some students may want to drip glue and sprinkle glitter over the newspaper.

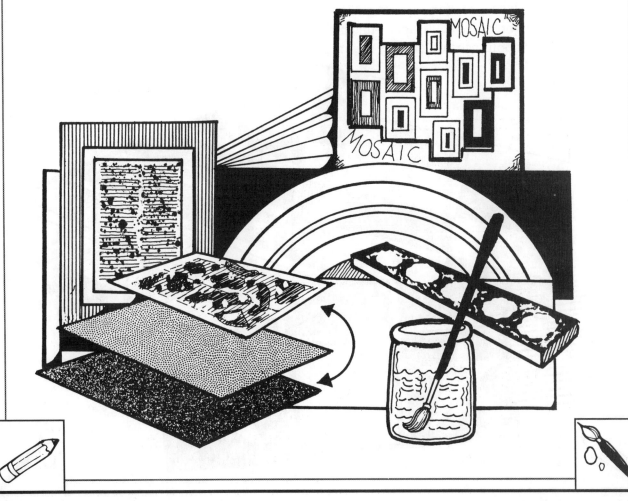

Patriotic Days

Materials

newspaper ad or coupon section; red and blue markers, pencils, or watercolors; scissors; glue; one 9" x 12" (23 cm x 30 cm) sheet of white construction paper per student; small self-sticking stars (optional)

Directions

1. Cut out large blocks of ads or store coupons, approximately 7" x 9" (15 cm x 18 cm). If possible, try to choose pages of store coupons or ads that are similar in size.

2. Have students color the boxed areas on the ad/coupon block, alternating colors to create patches of red and blue.

3. Add self-sticking red and blue stars if desired.

4. Glue the newspaper on the white construction paper.

   Note: When working on projects related to other countries, choose colors representative of those countries.

Extensions

- Use black construction paper to make silhouettes of patriotic symbols or people. Glue them on top of the newspaper. Attach stories about patriotic symbols, historic events, and/or famous patriots. Display the art and writing activities.

Butterfly Silhouettes

Materials

ad section of the newspaper about 7" (18 cm) square for each student; watercolors; scissors; glue; optional pattern (below); one 9" (23 cm) square black construction paper per student

Directions

1. Distribute the newspaper ad squares. Ask students to watercolor blocks of ads. Use a variety of bright colors. If necessary, add a second coat of watercolor to make colors more vivid. Let dry.

2. Create a border by gluing the newspaper on the square piece of black construction paper.

3. Using black construction paper, draw and cut out silhouettes of butterflies. Use the patterns below, if desired.

4. Put glue down the center of the butterfly silhouettes and mount them on the newspaper ad. When dry, pull the wings up to give the silhouettes a three-dimensional look.

   Note: Use other colors of construction paper for butterflies and mounting, if desired.

Extensions

- Add sequins or glitter to butterflies.
- Display the butterfly silhouettes when studying the life cycle of the butterfly.
- Replace the butterfly with silhouettes of other things from nature, such as flowers, birds, frogs. Have the class write haiku or other forms of poetry about their chosen silhouette.

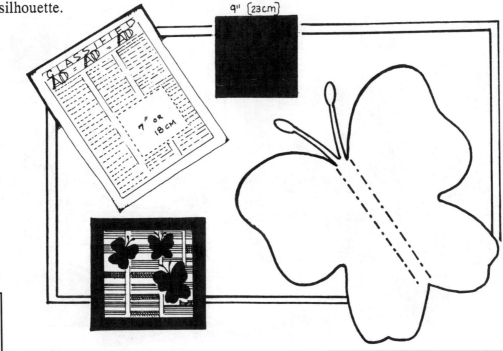

Holiday Trees

Materials

one 6" x 9" (15 cm x 23 cm) sheet of newspaper and one 6" x 9" (15 cm x 23 cm) sheet of green construction paper for each student; glue; hole punch; magazines; yarn or string; glitter or sequins (optional)

Directions

1. Have students fold the sheet of newspaper in half along the length. Draw half of the tree outline so that the center of the tree is against the fold.

2. Cut out the tree outline with it still folded.

3. Cut out slices of the tree as shown below. (You can save these for making geometric designs and other decorations.)

4. Open the tree pattern and glue it on green construction paper.

5. Punch holes in colorful pages of a magazine. Make ornaments for the tree by gluing on punched-out circles. Trim the tree with yarn or string (garland). If desired, add glitter and/or sequins.

Extensions

- Make a holiday card by stapling or gluing a piece of construction paper on the back of the newspaper art. Write a holiday greeting on the inside.

- Use the basic newspaper tree pattern to make a forest background for bulletin boards, signs, and displays about the effects of deforestation and the need for recycling wood products.

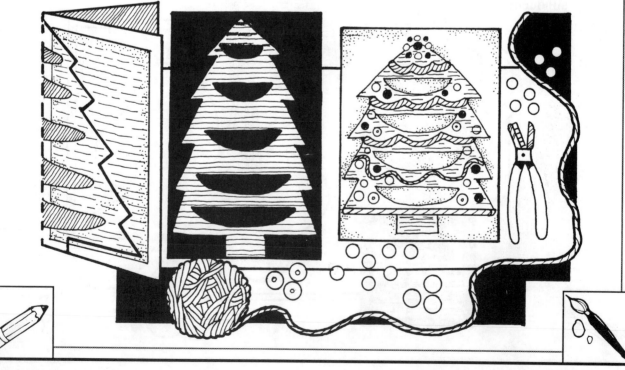

My Own Menu

Materials

school menu from newspaper or printed school menu; pens or pencils; watercolors or paints; fine point black markers; scissors; one 9" x 12" (23 cm x 30 cm) sheet of construction paper for each student; glue; paint brushes

Directions

1. Cut out the school menu from a newspaper.
2. Have students use the fine point marker to draw some favorite foods on the menu. Watercolor the inside of the food.
3. Center and glue the menu on a sheet of construction paper.

Extensions

- Use seasonal construction paper such as orange/black for Halloween, red/green for Christmas, and red/white/blue for patriotic celebrations. Draw holiday foods on the menu.
- Cut out food from grocery ads and glue them on the menu.
- Cut out class schedules and paint favorite subjects or activities on them. Mount the schedules on colorful construction paper.

Faces

Materials

newspaper; scissors; glue; markers; construction paper

Directions

1. Have students draw a silhouette or a full-face outline of a face.

2. Mount the face on a piece of construction paper and use it for one of the extension activities.

Extensions

- If you study famous people throughout the year or include current events in your daily/weekly schedule, have students draw and cut out silhouettes of "Faces in the News" and mount them on paper. The student can include a story or information about the famous person next to the silhouette.

- Younger students can draw a full-face outline. Add facial features. Glue the face on paper. Decorate it by adding yarn for hair, a hat made out of cloth and real feather, etc. Have students give their faces a name and personality. Ask them to share the faces with the class.

18

3-D Trees

Materials

watercolors or watercolor markers; two 9" x 12" (23 cm x 30 cm) pieces of construction paper for each student (green for tree, any color for frame); glue; scissors; classified ad section of the newspaper; medium point black markers; paint brushes

Directions

1. Cut a 7" x 10" (18 cm x 25 cm) rectangle from the newspaper ad section.

2. Color in some blocks of ads using a variety of different colors.

3. Outline the colored blocks with a medium point marker.

4. Glue the ad section to the center of construction paper (frame).

5. Make a 3-D Tree. Cut out a tree pattern (large irregular leaf section and a trunk section) and glue it to colored ads as shown. Cut two smaller leaf sections and glue the center sections to the center of the tree pattern's leaf section. (When dry, fold these sections out to create a 3-D effect.)

6. Fold edges of construction paper (about 1" / 2.54 cm) toward the ad to make a frame. Pinch and glue the corners.

Extensions

• Make 3-D frames for a variety of writing and other curricular activities.

Dinosaurs

Materials

white construction paper; scissors; newspaper; glue; dinosaur books or patterns (optional); yarn, string, or a coat hanger; craft sticks

Directions

1. Draw a favorite dinosaur on white paper. Use pre-made patterns if necessary. Cut out the dinosaur pattern and use the cut-out pattern to trace the dinosaur onto newspaper.

2. Cut out the newspaper dinosaur and glue it to the white paper dinosaur. Allow the glue to dry.

Extensions

• On the white construction paper side, write the name of the dinosaur and some facts about it. Hang the dinosaurs in the classroom or make dinosaur mobiles on hangers.

• Younger students can make stick puppets by gluing the bottom of the dinosaurs to craft sticks.

Newspaper Fans

Materials

newspaper, cut into a rectangular shape; scissors; yarn or ribbon; hole punch; watercolors; staple or tape; paint brushes

Directions

1. Watercolor a newspaper rectangle. Allow the paint to dry.

2. Fold the newspaper into a fan shape. With fan closed, tape or staple one end of the folds. Make a bow out of yarn and attach it to this end.

3. Punch a row of holes near the top of the fan and weave ribbon through the holes. Tape the end pieces. (Weave a second row, if desired.)

   Note: If students want to decorate the fans with glitter, sequins, etc., add these after step 1 above.

Extensions

- Have students make large newspaper fans. Ask them to write short "Fan Letters" to someone they admire from the past or present. Use paper that will adequately fit on an opened fan. Each student can then attach his or her letter to the front of the fan and display it on a wall or bulletin board.

Newspaper Trees

Materials

four double sheets of newspaper; scissors; extra newspaper; coffee cans or other containers

Directions

1. Spread out one sheet of newspaper and roll it up from the narrow end. Just before you reach the end, overlap another sheet to the end and continue rolling.

2. Continue the process until you have used all four pieces of newspaper.

3. Cut the top half of the roll into fourths. (See picture below.)

4. Hold the roll at the bottom and carefully pull the "branches" out from the top of the tree until it resembles the finished tree below.

5. "Plant" your tree in the container using the extra paper to secure it.

Extensions

- Use a collection of student-made trees to create a rainforest scene, cornstalks around a fall harvest or Thanksgiving display, or to add a tropical look to a reading area.

- Make them into word trees by attaching word cards to them. Words that fit a specific category can be placed on one tree with a label identifying the category attached to the container. (Students may want to make smaller trees to keep at their desks. They could add information cards on any topic they like.)

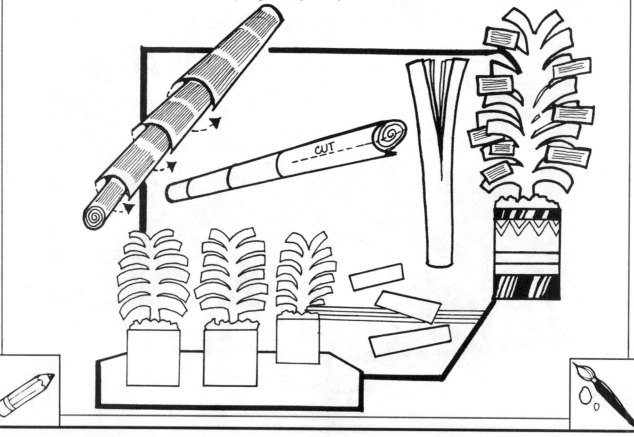

Accordion-Folded Newspaper Projects

Materials

scissors; newspaper; markers; stapler, glue, or tape; index paper; string; construction paper

Directions

To make standard accordion-folds:

1. Spread a full-sized sheet of newspaper on a working surface. Cut two narrow strips (about 1 ½"/ 4 cm wide) along the length of the newspaper.

2. Overlap two ends of each newspaper strip so that they are at right angles to each other. Staple, glue, or tape these two ends together.

3. Accordion-fold the strips for a pop-up card or crawly. Lift the bottom strip and fold it over at the edge of the top strip. The strip which was on top is now on the bottom. Lift this bottom strip and fold it as you did the first one.

4. Continue folding the bottom strip over the top one until the strip is completely woven. Attach the end pieces.

You can vary the width of the accordion-folded newspaper strips by changing the width of the strips. Student can attach several strips to make long woven newspaper chains.

To Make Crawlies:

1. Cut each strip narrower at one end by tapering it about one-third of the way from the end.

2. Starting at the wide end, accordion-fold the strips as in steps 2 through 4 above.

3. Have students decorate the faces of the crawlies to make worms, snakes, lizards (add pipe cleaner legs), etc.

Accordion-Folded
Newspaper Projects *(cont.)*

To Make Pop-up Cards:

• Fold a sheet of index paper in half. Decorate and/or write a greeting on the front cover. Have students glue small pictures, shapes, sayings, etc., to one end of the accordion-folded strips. (Use short strips for pop-up cards.) Glue the other end to the inside of a folded piece of index paper so that when it is opened, the card will pop up.

To Make Marionettes:

• Choose a character for the marionette. Cut out a head and torso pattern. Use accordion-folded newspaper strips for the arms and legs; add hands and feet. Attach string to the hands, feet, and head. Criss-cross two tongue depressors and tape them together at the center. Attach each piece of string from a limb to the end of one of the tongue depressors. Attach the string from the head to the center where the tongue depressors cross.

Nifty Names

Materials

newspaper; scissors; construction paper; homemade or commercial watercolors; glue; pens, pencils, or fine point markers

Directions

1. Using newspaper, have students measure and draw the letters of their name. (Younger children do better with tracing around pre-cut letters. Letter patterns are provided on pages 92-94.)
2. Watercolor over the drawn letters. Let them dry. Cut out letters.
3. Glue the letters on construction paper in any arrangement.

Extensions

- Place finished names on material or other background and display them with student writing.
- Have students bring in shoe boxes; decorate and glue the students' names to their boxes. Students can use the personalized boxes for supplies.

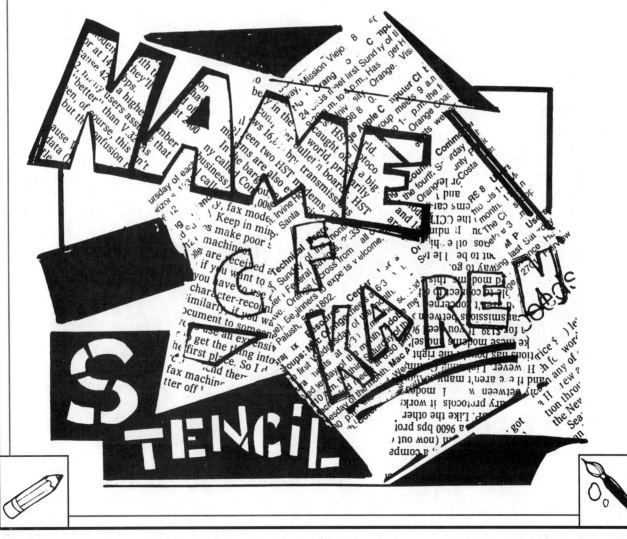

Creative Collages

Car Ads

Cut out car ads from the newspaper. Watercolor each and glue the ads onto a piece of construction paper or butcher paper. Give the collage a title. Have students write their own car advertisements or use the collage to design ad posters for a new car dealership. Older students can write math problems involving the car sales. Younger students can use the collages to identify similarities and differences between cars, car types, car parts, etc. If different types of land transportation are used in a collage, have students classify them by number of wheels, vehicle use, etc.

"In the News" Collage

Have students cut out newspaper articles relating to a specific subject or problem being studied in class. Glue the collected articles on a large piece of paper in a collage fashion. Add a title. Ask students to write related questions or main ideas for some of the articles in the collage.

Shapes Collage

Draw geometric shapes on sheets of newspaper. Cut them out and glue them on paper. Label each shape. Older students can add equations for finding the area, volume, or circumference of specific shapes. The collage can also be used as a visual reference. Ask younger students to refer to the collage for shape identification activities.

Face Collage

Have students cut out pictures of faces from magazines and newspapers. Mount them on a large piece of paper. Include as many ethnic groups as possible, as well as young and old faces. Have students write stories to accompany the collage. Choose a theme such as "We are Family" or "The Human Family."

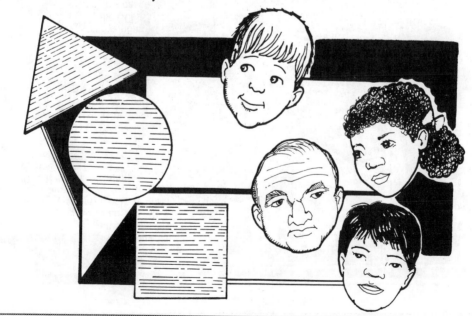

Newspaper Structures

Materials

newspaper; masking tape; scissors; string

Directions

For this project, students will be asked to make a structure out of newspaper. Working in small groups is an excellent way to foster creativity, and the added work force facilitates the assembly of the newspaper structures. Give students the freedom to choose the design of their structures. Only the materials provided can be used.

Have students practice rolling newspaper sheets for the structures they will build. Decide on an appropriate time limit in which to make the newspaper structures. Ask the groups to share their experience with the class.

Extensions

- Structures made from rolled newspaper are surprisingly strong. You can design specific structures such as bridges and towers, and use them for a variety of classroom activities.

Save the Environment and Save Pennies

In this section, students will be recycling materials to use for art projects. This is a good opportunity to discuss recycling and to encourage the students' participation in activities that build environmental awareness.

"Recycle Here" Center

- Set aside an area of the classroom for collection and storage of recycled items that will be used for the projects in this section. Do not limit yourself to the items listed. Encourage students to bring in other reusable items and determine ways in which they may be put to use.

- Give the recycling center a title. Using recycled paper, have students draw or find pictures of themselves and others engaging in activities to save our earth. Take photographs of school or community activities that involve recycling. Make posters that show the positive effects of recycling and display them at the collection center. Have students title the posters "Let's keep our earth clean and beautiful" or "Let's do our part to save the earth," or "This is how we recycle things," etc.

- A classroom recycling center will help students realize the importance of recycling as they learn ways to "pinch pennies."

Paint Savers

Materials

egg cartons; markers; several colors of tempera paint

Directions

1. Collect egg cartons throughout the year. Egg cartons can be used for art projects, games, and as storage containers throughout the year, so keep a supply on hand.

2. To use egg cartons for paint storage:

   • Provide several cartons for easy access to paint as it is needed for art projects.

   • Each student or group of students can have a paint carton. This makes distribution and preparation of materials for art projects much easier. Have students/groups write their names on the lids. If possible, store the paint cartons in a cabinet or at an art center.

   • For a painting activity, pour a different liquid tempera color in each cup. When students have finished painting, let the paint dry in the cup, close the lid and set the carton aside.

   • For the next paint activity, if paint remains in the cup, just add water and stir; if the cup is empty put more of same color in the cup.

Extensions

   • These cartons can be used throughout the year. Students can take home colorful egg cartons at the end of the school year.

   • You could also add extra paint, let it dry, and send the carton home for children to continue using during vacation months.

Paper Quilts

Materials

magazine pictures; scissors; large pieces of cardboard or heavy paper; glue; markers

Directions

1. Select colorful pictures from old magazines.

2. Cut circles, squares, triangles, or other geometric figures out of cardboard or heavy paper for stencil patterns.

3. Use stencil patterns to cut out magazine pictures in geometric shapes.

4. On a large piece of cardboard, arrange shapes into a quilt pattern. Show children how to overlap shapes.

5. Glue shapes to cardboard. Trim sides if any overlap.

6. With a marker draw tiny stitches to look as if it has been quilted.

Extensions

- Arrange pieces on a stocking pattern for Christmas. Add names, some holly with red berries, etc.

- Punch holes around the sides of each cardboard piece and "sew" several together with yarn for a large class quilt.

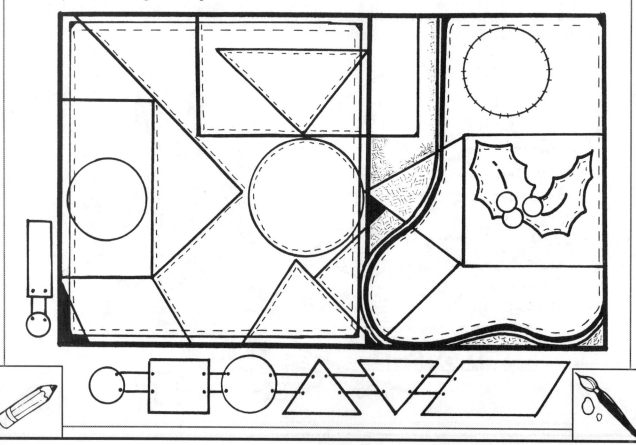

Bag Costumes

Materials

large brown grocery bags; scissors; string, belt, or yarn; markers, crayons, or paint

Directions

Top of Costume

1. Turn bag upside down. Cut a circular opening on top for the head.
2. Cut out openings on narrow sides of bag (near head) for arms.
3. Decorate the grocery bag for the character portrayed. Use markers, paints, crayons, buttons, and any other scrap materials available.

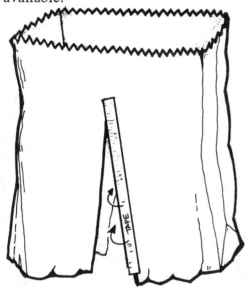

Bottom of Costume (pants)

1. Stand large grocery bag upright.
2. Cut bottom of bag completely off to put feet through.
3. Cut about halfway up each of the wide sides of the bag to form the legs. Tape along the inseam of the legs to close up.
4. Decorate for the character portrayed.
5. Put feet and legs in and pull up to waist.
6. Using string, yarn, or a belt, gather bag around waist.

Bottom of Costume (skirt)

1. Follow steps 1 and 2 for pants above.
2. Cut skirt to desired length.
3. Decorate for the character portrayed.
4. Gather at waist with a belt, string, or yarn.

Activities

• Use these bag costumes for school plays, to depict favorite book characters, and for a variety of other activities throughout the year. Children can take them home when completed. You may wish to store some in boxes for spontaneous activities as well. They can be easily folded and stored.

The Ocean Blue

Materials

white construction paper; blue construction or butcher paper; glue; scissors; crayons, markers, or watercolors; colored magazine pictures; plastic bubble packing material; paint brushes

Directions

1. On white paper, draw the pattern of a large fish.

2. Cut out the pattern and glue it on blue paper (ocean background).

3. Using crayons, markers, or watercolors, color the head, tail, fins the same color.

4. Cut out scales from colored magazine pictures and glue on fish.

5. With white crayon or chalk make waves on blue water.

6. Use the bubble packing material over pictures to create an ocean water appearance.

Extensions

- Make a class underwater scene using a large sheet of blue butcher paper and adding varieties of plant and sea life. Attach interesting fact cards about the plants and sea creatures.

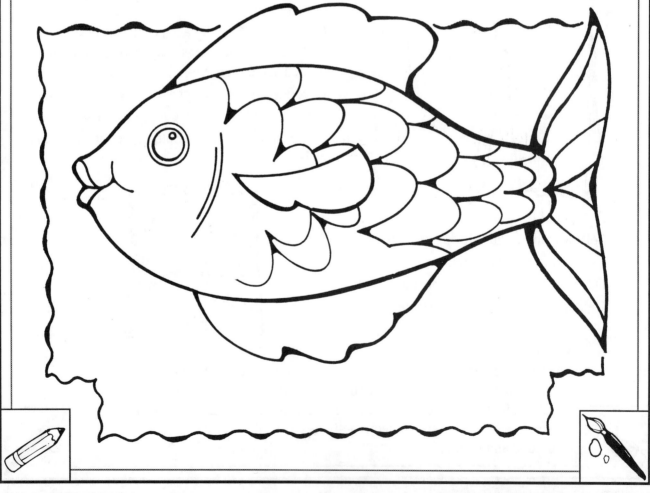

Egg Carton Characters

Materials

egg cartons; pipe cleaners; material scraps; sequins; buttons; markers or paints; scissors; glue, tape, or stapler

Directions

1. Cut the lid from the carton; save it to use later.

2. Cut 12 cups. (You may not need all of them.)

3. Decide on the characters (people, animals, something from a book).

4. Design the characters. Students can stack cups, add on bits of carton, material scraps, pipe cleaners, etc., to decorate their characters.

5. Use paint or markers to add features.

6. Set all characters on the lid to dry.

7. Ask students to share their egg carton characters.

Extensions

- Students can work in small groups to create characters they will use for a group display. They could recreate a story scene or write a new story about fictional characters they have created.

Crayon Art

Materials

old crayons; waxed paper; iron; newspaper; vegetable grater; construction paper; containers; old towel or piece of cloth

Directions

1. Place newspaper on a working surface. Collect an assortment of crayons that might otherwise be discarded. Separate the crayons into colors.

2. Use a vegetable grater to shave the crayons. Collect the shavings, by color, in the containers.

3. Decide on a pattern in which to put the crayon art (e.g., a simple construction paper frame, a bird shape, or a flower shape). Cut out two patterns from a piece of construction paper so that the pattern becomes a frame. (See picture below.)

4. Cut two sheets of waxed paper a little larger than the dimensions of the pattern you will be using.

5. Have students place one piece of waxed paper on the covered working surface and sprinkle some crayon shavings on the waxed paper. (Do not overfill the waxed paper surface or sprinkle shavings too close to the edge.)

6. Place the other piece of waxed paper over the crayon shavings and cover them with a towel or cloth. Melt the crayon shavings onto the sheets of waxed paper by using a warm iron.

7. Use the pattern frame as a stencil and cut the waxed paper/crayon design to fit the frame. "Sandwich" the waxed paper design between the two frames and glue it in place.

Extensions

- Display this colorful art by attaching thread or string to the tops of the creations and hanging them around the room. Or, place them on windows for a stained glass effect.

Lacy Butterflies

Materials

lace remnants; scissors; white thread or string; pipe cleaners

Directions

1. Cut out two lace rectangles, each about 2" x 5" (5 cm x 13 cm). Round the corners.

2. Holding the lace pieces horizontally, pinch the centers of each together to form the two sets of wings.

3. Wrap thread or string around the pinched center a few times and tie it tightly.

4. Bend a small pipe cleaner in half over the thread and shape it to look like antennas.

Extensions

• For variation, students can add sequins or use colored lace.

• Glue lace butterflies on the cover or inside of a thank-you or special-occasion card.

• Make gift boxes from sturdy boxes (with covers). Cover the boxes with wallpaper remnants. Attach one or two lacy butterflies to the gift box cover.

Milk Carton Art

Materials

small milk cartons (Collect milk cartons from students.); newspaper, construction paper, wallpaper, or contact paper remnants; scissors; crayons, markers, or paints; string or yarn; glue or tape; hole punch

Directions

1. Before starting a project, be sure that milk cartons have been cleaned and allowed to dry for a few days.

2. Open the carton along the top seam. Cover all surfaces with construction paper, wallpaper, or contact paper.

3. Using a theme or activity appropriate for the grade level or curriculum, have students design a carton display. Place the title of the carton art on the top section of the carton. Have students cut out or draw pictures to represent the title on the sides and bottom of the carton.

4. Punch a hole in the center of the carton's top seam. Attach a piece of yarn or string to the carton and suspend it on a wire, clothesline, or on hangers around the room. Students can also keep their carton art at their desks or at a center.

Extensions

• Write a five-verse or five-line poem using each side (surface) of the carton. Title the poem on the top portion of the carton.

• Flatten the top of the carton. Have students cover all surfaces with newspaper, wallpaper, material, contact paper, or construction paper. The covered cartons can be used as building blocks for many projects.

• Make a house from each carton. Choose a texture for the exterior, such as red or yellow construction paper for bricks, another color for painted wood, etc. Draw bricks or wood and glue the textured exterior all around the milk carton. Add a roof and other exterior features. Assemble several houses into a town or village.

Decorated Pie Plates

Materials

nail and hammer; styrofoam tray or heavy cardboard; paper; marker or pencil; aluminum pie plate; tape; glue or glue gun

Directions

1. On construction paper, have students design a caption or illustration for their pie plate decorations.

2. Place the paper over the inside surface of the aluminum pie plate and secure it with tape.

3. Place the styrofoam tray or cardboard on a work surface. Lay the pie plate on top of the styrofoam tray. Use a hammer and nail to punch holes along the design lines on the paper and through the pie plate. The styrofoam tray facilitates the hole punching and serves to protect the work surface. Remove the paper and enjoy your design!

Note: The use of a hammer and nails should be supervised by an adult. Have younger children make simple designs or drawings on paper. Then have an adult or older "buddy" punch the holes in the pie plate.

Extensions

- Decorate the pie plates by adding trim to the edge. Punch a hole at the top of the plate, add string, yarn, or ribbon and hang the decorated pie plate on a wall.

- Use decorated pie plates as gifts.

- Make them into plaques.

- Punch numbers, letters, or words on plates and use them for classroom activities.

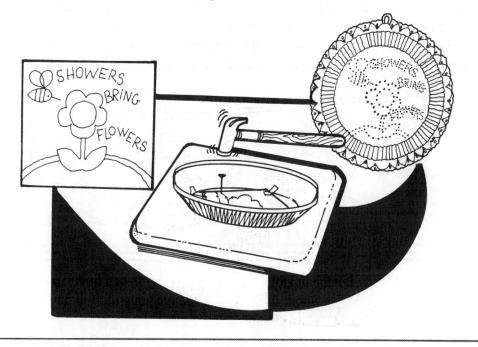

Reusable Tubes

Materials

toilet tissue or paper towel tubes; a supply of one or more of the following—magazine pictures, yarn, string, ribbon, newspaper, fabric remnants, construction paper, paint, markers, tissue paper; glue; tape; scissors

Tube Projects

• Use toilet tissue or paper towel tubes to make the projects below and on page 39.

Tube Mailers

• Decorate the outside of the tube with bits of colored magazine pictures or pieces of newspaper. Have each student write a note, letter, or reminder on paper, roll it up, insert it in the tube mailers, and send it to another class member.

• Have students make their own awards, place them in the decorated tubes, and present them to a special person.

Marble Run

• Have students work in groups to create a marble run using a series of tubes connected to form a kind of chute. Use masking tape to connect the tubes. Encourage students to design the most unique or fastest marble run they can. Have students share their marble runs with the class, explaining how they made their designs and the problems and/or successes they experienced.

Reusable Tubes *(cont.)*

Tube Treats

- Fill tubes with small gift items, treats, a small reward or certificate, etc. Cut a sheet of tissue paper about 5" (13 cm) longer than the length of the tube. Wrap the tube in tissue, leaving excess tissue on each side. Tie the ends of the tube with yarn, string, or ribbon.

Tube People

- Have students draw facial features on the tube. Paint or color the features and add yarn and other materials to complete the face. Have students place fingers inside the tubes and use as finger puppets.

- Make entire tube people figures by adding clothing and accessories.

- Tube people make interesting three-dimensional displays for bulletin boards.

Suggestions for Styrofoam

Igloos

- Pour white styrofoam packing material in a large open box. Draw a circle on a piece of cardboard. Glue white styrofoam packing material around the circle line.

- Put glue on top of the first row of packing material and start another row. (Set this row in a little toward the middle.) Continue adding rows in this way until the pieces meet at the top in a dome shape.

- When the igloo is dry, use black marker and draw a door.

- **Note**: Younger children will probably need assistance getting started with this project.

Styrofoam Letters, Designs, and Structures

- Have students write letters or words on cardboard or heavy stock paper. Spread glue over the letters and press pieces of styrofoam on the glue.

- Styrofoam letters can be used for bulletin board titles, students' names, and displays.

- Styrofoam can be cut into interesting three-dimensional designs. Create and paint styrofoam designs or structures for a display.

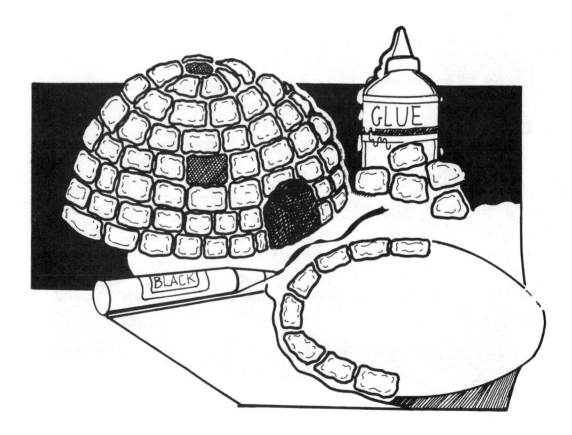

Suggestions for Styrofoam *(cont.)*

Fast Food Boxes

Collect sectioned styrofoam boxes (with attached lids) from fast food restaurants. Try the following projects.

- Have students cut out pictures relating to a theme, area of interest, category, etc. Glue them in the sections of the fast food box. Make a title card and glue it to the cover. These can be displayed at a center for students to use or attached as a three-dimensional display to a bulletin board.

- Collect objects that can be used for classification. Write a title and directions on an index card and attach it to the cover. Place items to be sorted in a sealable bag. Students can use the fast food boxes over and over again by changing the activity card and sorting objects.

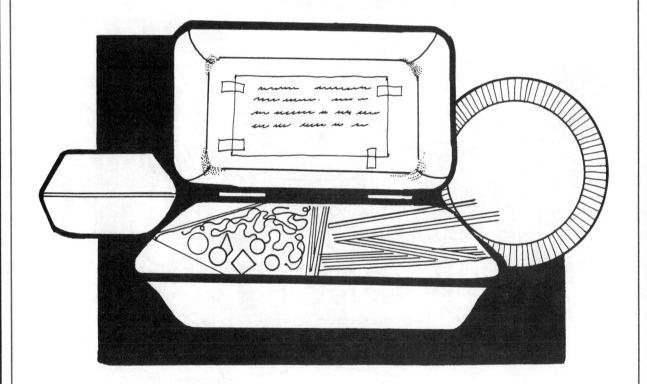

Junk Boxes

Materials

shoe boxes; materials for decorating boxes—markers, paint, paper or material scraps, pictures, cut-out letters, etc.; scissors; glue

Directions

1. Have students decorate the outside surfaces of the shoe box (including the lid). They may want to personalize their junk boxes by adding their names. A set of letter stencils is provided on pages 92-94.

2. Fill the boxes with school supplies such as glue, scissors, extra pencils, erasers, crayons, and resealable plastic bags (for small objects such as math manipulatives).

Extensions

*   Decorate shoe boxes for general classroom use. During the year, drop in leftover art materials for children to use for creative projects.

Patriotic Windsocks

Materials

toilet tissue, paper towel, or wrapping paper tubes; paper; newspaper; red, white, and blue watercolors, paints, or markers; scissors; string or yarn; hole punch; glue or tape

Directions

1. Use watercolors, paints, or markers to color tubes with red, white, and blue stripes or designs. Cut out star shapes from aluminum foil and glue them to the tube.

2. Make streamers by cutting 1" x 24" (about 3 cm x 60 cm) strips of newspaper and attaching them to the bottom end of the tube. Students can color or paint the strips.

3. Punch three or four holes near the top of the tube. Tie a piece of yarn or string to each hole. Bring the yarn or string up evenly and tie them together. Hang the windsocks near a window or doorway. If possible, take them outside and attach them to a tree.

Extensions

• Make patriotic windsocks for Veterans' Day, Memorial Day, or the Fourth of July. Replace newspaper streamers with red, white, and blue paper streamers. Have students write the names of patriots or familiar patriotic expressions on the streamers.

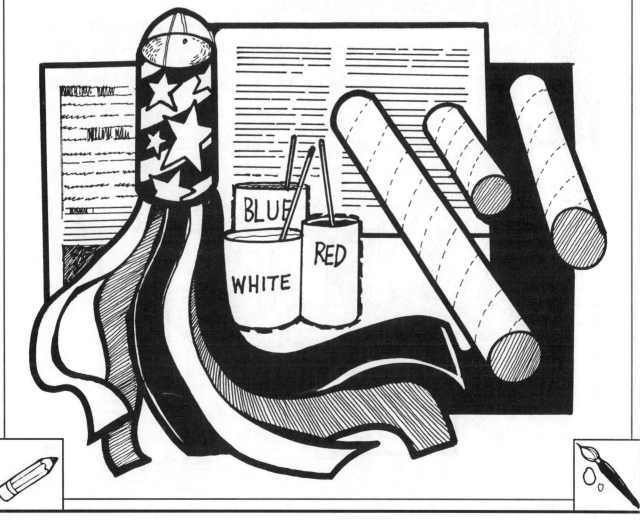

Card Mobiles

Materials

old or used greeting cards; scissors; construction paper; yarn or string; hangers; hole punch

Directions

1. Cut out some pictures from greeting cards. The pictures should reflect a theme or topic about which the students will write a poem or story.

2. Punch a hole at the top of each picture.

3. Tie string or yarn to the hole and attach the other end of the string to the hanger.

4. Cut a rectangular piece of construction paper to fit inside the hanger. On the paper, have students write poems or short stories about the set of pictures they have chosen.

5. Punch holes in the corners of the construction paper. Tie yarn or string to the holes and attach the paper to the hanger. (Note: To use lined paper for writing, cut a rectangular piece of lined writing paper about the same size as the construction paper and ask students to write their poems or stories on it. Glue the finished poems/stories on the construction paper.)

Extensions

- Cut out a large assortment of pictures from greeting cards. Store them in a box. Hang several pieces of yarn from the hanger and attach a large paper clip to the end of each piece. Attach a blank sign for the center of the hanger using the directions in steps 4 and 5 above. Choose greeting card pictures that are related in some way to the hanging yarn or string. Clip them to the yarn/string.

- Use the mobile for a variety of activities in which the students try to connect the pictures to a title or activity you have written in the center of the hanger.

- Change the cards and titles regularly and encourage students to find solutions to the activities.

Shamrock Quilts

Materials

various colors of construction paper, including green; scissors; markers; crayons; glue; butcher paper

Directions

1. Fold and cut out three identical large green hearts.

2. Draw a black line down the center of each heart.

3. Cut out a green stem.

4. Using markers or crayons, make a pattern or design. Be sure to make each half differently.

5. Glue the hearts together to make a shamrock. (See picture below.)

6. Have children glue their shamrocks to different color squares of construction paper. Make a quilt by gluing the shamrock squares in a quilt pattern to a large piece of butcher paper. With markers, draw stitches connecting the shamrock squares.

Extensions

- Use other materials such as fabric or wallpaper scraps to cover each half of the hearts.
- Change the shamrock into a flower by adding one or two more hearts to form the petals of the flower. Add a stem and leaves.

Egg Carton Wreaths

Materials

paper plates; scissors; egg cartons; tempera paints; paint brushes; glue; ribbon; glitter

Directions

1. Cut the center circle from a paper plate (any size). Store the cut-out circles for other art projects where you might need a circle shape.

2. Paint the ring green. Allow it to dry.

3. Cut off the lid of the egg carton. The lids can be used for storing materials such as scissors, pencils and crayons, or manipulatives at centers or desks.

4. Cut out each of the cups. Carefully cut slits around the top of each cup and spread the slit sections out to form petals.

5. Dip the petals in tempera paint. (Choose flower colors.) Allow the petals to dry.

6. Glue the bottom of each egg carton flower on the paper plate ring until it is covered with flowers.

7. Put a drop of glue inside each flower and sprinkle some glitter in the center. Allow it to dry.

8. Add a colorful bow made from ribbon or construction paper.

Extensions

- Wreaths can be made as decorations for many occasions. Use the paper plate rings as the foundation for the wreath. For Christmas, cut green tissue into small strips. Twist each strip in the middle. Glue the twist to the ring. Fill the entire ring with tissue twists. Add other holiday decorations and glitter.

- Display colorful wreaths around the room with students' work, illustrations, photos, etc., in the centers of the wreaths.

Store Simulations

Materials

empty boxes and cans that have contained food; grocery bags; large paper scraps for signs, labels, etc.; markers; pencils; play money; calculators (optional)

Directions

1. Be sure boxes, cans, cartons, etc., are cleaned. Check items for sharp edges.

2. Brainstorm with students the tasks and materials they need to consider when owning or managing a store.

3. Set up a store in the classroom. Have students categorize the items and arrange them by section in their store.

4. Make signs, price labels, etc.

Extensions

- This is a wonderful way to teach math or nutrition.

- Assign students to be clerks, cashiers, and customers. Alternate jobs so that each student has an opportunity to experience more than one role.

- Set up a check-out counter. Use play money. If possible, bring in a toy cash register and some calculators. As the cashier calculates the charges, the clerk bags the groceries.

- As an alternative to the grocery store, set up a clothing store. Have students bring in clothes that are intended for donation to a community organization or a school clothing drive. Students can price and purchase the items in their store simulation activities. When done, box the clothing for donation to a favorite organization.

Tear Art

Materials

tag board or cardboard; scraps of art tissue, construction paper, newspaper, magazines; glue; paper; pencils; marker; egg carton tops (optional)

Directions

1. Create a scene on a piece of tag board or cardboard. (For this project it is suggested that scenes be simple and some large areas on which to glue torn pieces of paper be provided.) Tear pieces of art tissue paper, construction paper, newspaper, magazines, etc. Store them in an egg carton top, if available.

2. Glue the torn pieces to the tagboard or cardboard. Choose an area of the scene—a grassy hill, for example—and glue torn green art tissue to it. Then glue another section with another color or a different kind of torn paper.

Extensions

- When the scenes are complete, have students write stories or poems about them. Share the art and writing experiences in class.

- Make use of paper that is worn around the edges.

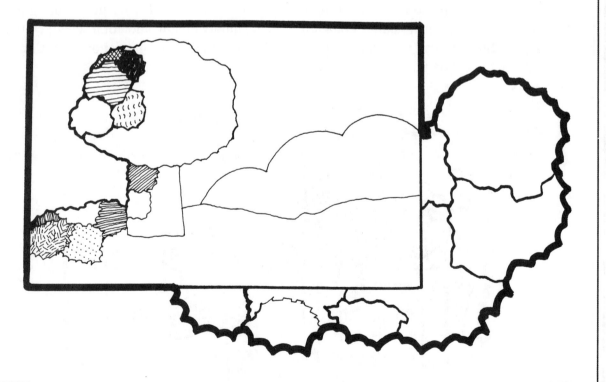

Box and Tube Castles

Materials

cardboard boxes; paper towel tubes; tape; tempera paints; string; scissors or craft knives; glue

Directions

1. Cut off the top of the box. Use the top to make a roof (step 6). All around the top of the box, cut evenly spaced slits about one-fourth of the way down. Push in every other set of slits to form the notched tops of the castle walls.

2. Make a drawbridge by cutting the sides and top of a door opening, leaving the bottom of the door uncut.

3. Poke two holes in the wall above the drawbridge opening and two holes in the top corners of the drawbridge. Thread a piece of string through the opened drawbridge to the top holes in the wall and back through the other hole in the drawbridge. Knot the ends of the string.

4. Create towers from four paper towel tubes. Cut slits at one end of each tube and push in as in step 1.

5. Position the towers as shown below and glue the tubes to the castle. Allow the glue to dry.

6. To make a roof, tape or glue the carton top on the folded-in tabs.

7. Cut out or paint castle windows. Paint the castle.

Extensions

- Have several groups make box and tube castles. Create a three-dimensional medieval scene complete with feudal villages.

- Use a box and tube castle as part of a center for books and stories about dragons, kings and knights, etc.

Computer Paper Edges

Form-feed computer paper edges can be used for a variety of curricular activities. Collect and store a supply of paper edges to use throughout the year. If possible, obtain a variety of colors.

Materials

dot matrix printer computer paper edges, a variety of colors, if available; glue; construction paper; paint or markers when applicable

Use computer paper edges for the following projects:

- Make rings for decorative chains to be used at a party or other special occasions. Cut computer edges into shorter strips. Make a ring shape from one strip and glue the ends together. Slip another strip through the ring and glue its ends together. Continue until you reach a desired length. (Chain rings can be made the same size by counting a specific number of holes before cutting.)

- If possible, use a variety of colors for a more festive look. Make red and green chains for Christmas. Use red, white, and blue chains for patriotic holidays.

- Create a decorative frame for a picture, students' writing, etc. Have students leave space around the art or writing project. Make a frame by gluing a single or double frame of computer paper edges around the project being framed.

- Use the computer paper holes for a math lesson in counting groups of 5's, 10's, etc. Since the holes in standard dot matrix printer computer paper are $\frac{1}{2}$ inch (1.25 cm) apart, the paper edges can be used for standard measurement activities involving U.S. customary measurements. Younger students can also measure objects and make comparisons using the paper edges as a non-standard measuring tool.

- Make pictures with computer paper edges. Draw an object or simple design on a piece of construction paper or cardboard. Glue paper edges over the line drawing. Color or paint the inside sections of the picture.

- Prepare block letter names, display labels, or bulletin board titles using strips of computer paper edges to form block letters. This is an easy and economical way to label projects, centers, etc.

50

Bottle Terrariums

Materials

two-liter plastic soda bottles; metal spoons or butter knives; craft knife; aluminum foil; small rocks or pebbles; enriched soil; plants; water; insects (optional)

Directions

1. With a spoon or knife, carefully pry the bottle from its base.

2. Using a craft knife, cut off the bottom three inches (8 cm) from the bottle. Set the plastic bottle aside. (Rather than discarding the cut-off section use it as a classroom storage container.)

3. Line the bottom and sides of the base with foil. Place a few small rocks or pebbles inside the container. Half-fill the container with soil. Set plants in soil and continue to fill the base with soil until the soil level reaches about one inch (about 3 cm) below the rim.

4. Add insects and/or decorative rocks or twigs. Water soil until moist.

5. Cover the soil section with the plastic bottle, fitting its bottom edge inside the rim of the soil section. Re-cap the bottle tightly. (If a cap is not available, cover the bottle with a small piece of foil.)

6. Place the terrarium in a sunny area but not in direct sunlight. Add a few drops of water periodically if the soil seems to be getting dry.

Extensions

• Add insects to the terrariums. Use the terrariums to study plant and animal life.

Santa's Reindeer

Materials

tall plastic, cardboard, or metal cans (with lids); brown construction paper; red, white, and green felt scraps (Substitute with construction paper if necessary.); scissors; measuring tape; glue; tape

Directions

1. Cover the can with brown construction paper. Tape or glue the edges together.

2. To make antlers, have students trace their hands on brown construction paper. Make two antlers.

3. Draw and cut two brown paper ears. Cut two small white felt ears and glue them inside the brown ears.

4. For the head, cut a brown strip of paper 3" (8 cm) wide and 14" (36 cm) long. Fold it in half. Trim the two corners opposite the fold by making a 45 degree cut. Glue the head near the top of the can. (The fold should be just under the lid, and the flap should hang loose.)

5. Draw two white oval eyes. Color the pupils black. Glue the eyes on the head flap.

6. Cut a large round nose from red felt and glue it under the eyes.

7. Glue an ear on each side of the face; glue the antlers behind the ears.

8. Cut holly from green felt, berries from red felt, and a bell from white felt. Glue these along the bottom of the can.

    Hint: Felt may be too hard for younger children to cut. Send the pattern home or have an older partner assist with the cutting.

Extensions

*   Use the reindeer for holiday decorations, fill with holiday treats, or use them as holiday mailboxes for student-created greeting cards, letters to Santa, etc.

*   Decorate cans with animals about which students are learning. Have students write facts, stories, poems, etc., about the animals, roll the papers up, and place them in the can for others to read and enjoy.

Spool Prints

Materials

large empty thread spools; pencils, thin wooden dowels or knitting needles (Choose an item with a diameter that will allow it to fit through the center hole of the spool.); non-hardening clay; craft sticks or sharpened pencils; old baking trays or styrofoam trays; construction paper or index paper cut to desired size; tempera paints; scissors; soap, water, and paper towels for clean-up

Directions

1. Prepare rollers by first covering the surface of the empty spool with about ¹/₂" (about 1.5 cm) layer of clay. Smooth the surface of the clay as much as possible and check to see if the clay is approximately the same thickness all around.

2. Push the pencil, wooden dowel, or knitting needle through the center hole in the spool.

3. Have students make patterns on the roller by pressing designs into the clay with a sharpened pencil or a craft stick. (For finer impressions use the end of a paper clip.)

4. Pour tempera paints into the baking tray or styrofoam tray. Hold the ends of the spool roller and roll it back and forth across the paint until the entire clay surface of the roller is covered with paint. The roller is ready to use.

Extensions

- Create a design on paper by pushing the roller across the paper in the area where you want the design to appear. Spool prints can be used to border welcome cards, bulletin boards, or students' work. To use more than one print color on a piece of paper, wash the paint off the roller with soap and water and pat it dry with a paper towel before each new color is added. Wait until one paint is dry before adding another.

Mushroom Prints

Materials

ripe, store-bought mushrooms (Provide enough mushrooms so that each student will have at least one. If possible, use mushrooms with large caps.); sheets of white paper (one per student); plastic cups or containers (one per student)

Directions

1. Divide the class into small groups. Distribute mushrooms, paper, and plastic cups/containers to students.

2. Ask students to look closely at the "wheel spokes" pattern on the underside of the mushroom caps. This pattern is produced by the gills. Carefully break off the stalk (stem) of the mushroom.

3. With the gill side down, place the mushroom on a white piece of paper and cover it and the paper with the cup/container. Leave the mushroom cap covered for about three hours.

4. Gently lift the cup or container off the paper. Remove the mushroom cap and observe what has happened—the spores which have fallen from the gills produced a "wheel spokes" pattern.

Extensions

• Students enjoy making these spore prints and will probably want to make more. Invite them to make their spore print patterns into a work of art.

• You may wish to extend your exploration of nature's art by preparing mushroom omelettes, cream of mushroom soup, or other easy-to-prepare mushroom dishes in class.

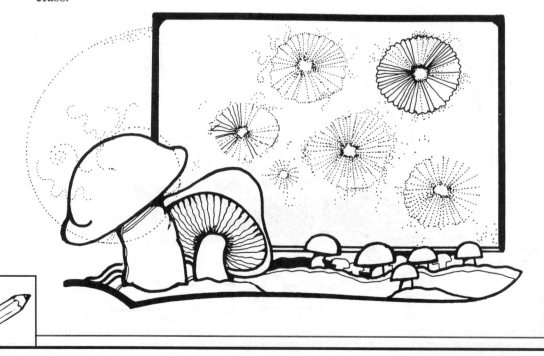

Pressed Wild Flowers

Materials

non-poisonous wild flowers; bright colored construction paper; colored cellophane paper; scissors; black construction paper; glue

Directions

1. Gather non-poisonous wild flowers. (Queen Anne's Lace is excellent.)

2. Press flowers between book pages for several days.

3. Remove the flowers from the book, carefully cut them to an appropriate size, and glue the flowers on a piece of brightly colored construction paper. Allow the glue to dry.

4. Cover the entire piece of construction paper with a sheet of cellophane paper and glue the edges of both pieces of paper together.

5. Make a frame from black construction paper and glue it to the cellophane.

Extensions

• For a three-dimensional effect, replace the pressed flowers with twigs, leaves, and grass. Do not add the cellophane covering. Frame the picture as in step 5.

• Display framed wild flowers around the room or on windows. Have students write about the flowers or how they picked and assembled the framed flowers. Write haiku or other poetry about nature.

Dried Flower Arrangements

Materials

wild flowers or other fresh-cut flowers; nails, wire, string, or coat hangers; scissors; a warm, dry, clean, airy, dark place for hanging flowers to dry

Directions

1. Cut the flowers just before they are in full bloom and remove the leaves.

2. Group flower families together, using a string or rubber band to tie their stems together. Be sure not to smash the blossoms tightly together because air must be able to circulate around the petals to thoroughly dry the blossoms in their original shape.

3. Hang the flower groupings upside-down, suspended from a nail, wire, string, or coat hanger. They will dry in three to five weeks.

Extensions

- Dried flower arrangements can be used to decorate tables at a school or class function.

- Make a bouquet by arranging a variety of dried flowers, tying them together, and adding a decorative ribbon. Create dried flower bouquets as gifts.

56

Cornhusk Dolls

Materials

cornhusks (available in grocery stores in Mexican food sections); string or yellow yarn; paints; scissors; paper towels; bucket or pan for soaking cornhusks; cloth or sponge; cotton, fabric or yarn (optional)

Directions

1. The husk is the foliage of the corn or maize plant that wraps the ear tightly in a protective coat. Cornhusks are tough. They can be braided, wrapped, twisted, and knotted.

   Prepare the husks by soaking them in warm water until they are soft (up to one hour). Drain husks on paper towels. Keep the husks damp with a cloth or sponge while working with them.

2. Put six cornhusks together and tie a string around the middle for the doll's waist. Tie another piece of string about 2" (5 cm) below the first to form the body. Fold the ends of the husks down from the top and hold them down by tying them in place with another string placed on top of the first string that was tied in the middle.

3. To form the arms and hands, put two husks together and tie them near the ends with strings. Roll and slip the arms through the opening in the top of the body near the neck, or tie the arms to the body by wrapping string around them at the neck.

4. For a skirt, keep the bottom of the dress as is. To make pants, divide or cut the husks below the waist. To form the legs and feet, roll the divided husks into trouser legs and tie them with string near the bottom.

5. Paint a face and clothing on the doll. If scraps of fabric are available, sew or glue them on the doll. Add hair by gluing paper strips, cotton, yarn, or fabric to the head.

Extensions

- Use cornhusk dolls for autumn displays.
- Have students learn about the origin of the cornhusk doll and incorporate it in a social studies lesson.

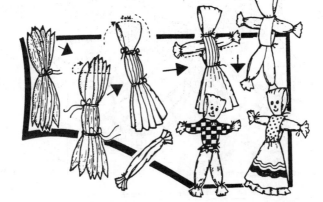

Pine Cones for the Holidays

Pine cones can be used in the making of projects or as part of the materials used for preparing art projects. Gather a variety of pine cones so that students will have a choice of size and/or shape when doing the following activities.

Christmas Pine Cones

- Make pine cone prints by dipping the base of a pine cone in tempera paint and rolling the paint-covered area of the pine cone on paper. Dip some pine cones in red paint and some in green paint.
- String out bits of cotton on pine cones. Sprinkle them with silver glitter. Use the decorated pine cones for a table centerpiece or to create a winter scene.
- Make pine cone wreaths and decorate them with holiday ribbon and ornaments.

Thanksgiving Turkeys

- Use a large pine cone for the body of the turkey. Add feathers (real or cut from construction paper) by gluing them in a circle to the base of the pine cone.
- To make the head, dip a styrofoam ball into brown paint and allow it to dry. Glue the ball to the other end of pine cone.
- Cut eyes, mouth, and nose from flannel scraps and glue them on the head.
- Cut a section of red pipe cleaner and glue it on the head. (Color a white pipe cleaner with red marker, if a red pipe cleaner is unavailable.)
- Shape pipe cleaners for feet.

Holiday Candles

- To make candles and holder you will need to collect the following: round-shaped pine cones, toilet tissue tubes, and small foil pans.
- Cover a toilet tissue tube with red, green, silver, or gold paper.
- Put glue in bottom of a foil pan. Place the toilet tissue tube in the center of the pan. Arrange pine cones around the base of the tube. Fill the tube with newspaper until it is stuffed. Cut a flame shape from construction paper and glue it to the top of the tube.
- Sprinkle glitter (silver or gold) on pine cones or put tiny red or green ribbons on pine cones if desired.

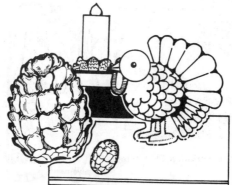

Plant Rubbing Collages

Materials

flowers, leaves, grass, or bark; light-weight white paper (not construction paper); crayons; newspaper; construction paper (any color); glue

Directions

1. Collect a variety of leaves, grasses, tree bark, woody stems, and flowers and distribute them so that each student has an assortment of plants from which to make rubbings.

2. Cover the working surface with newspaper to make clean-up easier.

3. Choose a plant for the first rubbing and cover it with a piece of light-weight white paper.

4. Using a crayon, rub over the surface of the paper that covers the plant. (For best results, have students rub the crayon on its side.)

5. Cut out design made by the plant rubbing and glue it on construction paper.

6. Choose another plant from the assortment and follow steps 3 through 5. Continue mounting plant rubbings until the collage is complete.

Extensions

- Use the activity to teach the different kinds of leaves, flowers, etc.

- Make autumn leaves by using orange, green, yellow, red, and brown crayons.

- Replace crayons with pencils to create an outline of the plant and fill the plant parts with watercolor.

Pussy Willow Displays

Materials

pussy willows; construction paper or index paper; markers, watercolors, crayons, or colorful tissue paper scraps; stapler; glue

Directions

1. Have students make a vase for the pussy willows. Decorate one side of a 9" x 12" (23 cm x 30 cm) piece of construction paper or index paper. Students can draw designs on the paper or glue tissue paper scraps in a collage design.

2. To make the vase, hold the paper lengthwise and form a cone shape. Glue the seams together.

3. Staple the students' vases to a large bulletin board.

4. Arrange some pussy willows in each vase. Allow some pussy willows to extend from the sides and top of each vase.

Extensions

- Arrange a display of student poems, stories, etc. (Leave adequate space between vases for students' work.)

Vases of pussy willows
all in the air
Beautiful pictures looking
so fair.
....susie

Egg Carton Gardens

Materials

cattails (or any wild flower with a stem); egg cartons; glue; scissors; green paint; green construction paper; pencil

Directions

1. Remove the egg carton lid. Cut the cup section in half.

2. Turn the carton half upside down (cups facing down).

3. Paint the upside down carton green.

4. Make a thin strip of grass from green construction paper to cover all sides at the base of the carton. Glue the grass around the bottom of carton.

5. With a pencil, punch a hole in the top of each egg carton cup and insert cattails.

6. Cut out petal shapes from the leftover egg carton cups. Use the petals to make little flowers.

7. Decorate the flowers with green leaves (cut from construction paper) and glue them inside the grass border near the bottom of the cattails.

Extensions

- Use flower arrangements as centerpieces for special classroom activities. Make arrangements as gifts. Place flower arrangements at a science or writing center while studying about plants.

Autumn Centerpieces

Materials

acorns; red, green, yellow, orange, and brown construction paper; pencils; black markers; large plastic lid or round piece of cardboard; glue; scissors; baby's breath (optional)

Directions

1. On construction paper, have students outline one of their hands (and part of the arm) to create a leaf pattern. Use a variety of fall colors to make the patterns.

2. Cut out the patterns and draw leaf veins with a marker.

3. Using a plastic lid or cardboard, arrange leaves along the perimeter, leaving an opening in the center. (Use the arm section of the pattern as a tab. Turn it under and glue it to the lid or cardboard base.) The hand pattern leaves should stand up.

4. Arrange acorns in the center of the circular pattern of leaves.

5. Fill in areas of the acorn center with Baby's Breath.

Extensions

• If your classroom has centers/stations or is arranged by tables or cooperative groups, place a centerpiece at each area. To identify the type of center, names of group members, etc., prepare signs for each centerpiece. (Suggestion: Make signs using directions for "Attention Getters" on page 74. Glue the craft stick in the middle of the centerpiece, between some acorns.)

62

Leaf Printing

Materials

a variety of leaves; tempera paints; large foil pan or tray; newspaper; construction paper; soap, water, and paper towels (for clean-up); rolling pin and waxed paper (optional)

Directions

1. Cover work surface with newspaper.

2. Pour liquid tempera paint into a large foil pan or tray.

3. Carefully lay a leaf on the surface of the paint.

4. Lift the leaf out of the paint and let the excess paint drip off.

5. With the paint side facing down, press the leaf on a piece of construction paper. (For a more crisp print, place waxed paper on top of the leaf and move a rolling pin back and forth across the waxed paper.)

6. When the leaf print dries, cut out the pattern.

Extensions

- Use a variety of paints and leaf designs. Have each student make several leaf prints. Cut out the prints and mount each on a separate piece of paper. Add information about the type of leaf/tree represented on each page. Each student can make an individual leaf book. Or, combine students' pages into a class book.

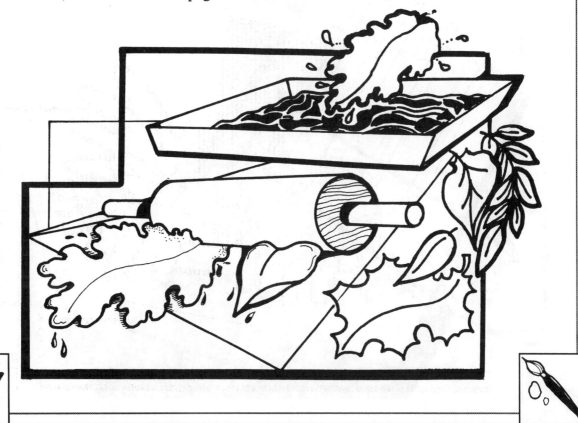

Around the Kitchen

Materials

kitchen utensils (no sharp objects); light-colored construction paper; pencils, markers, or crayons; tempera or watercolor paint; scissors

Directions

1. Have children bring in kitchen utensils. Discuss the function of each.

2. Place a variety of utensils on construction paper.

3. Using a pencil, marker, or crayon outline each utensil. (Overlap utensils.)

4. Paint kitchen items with tempera or watercolor paints. (Substitute paints with crayons, if desired.)

Extensions

- Cut out the utensils and mount them on paper.
- Cut strips of butcher paper. Have students design and color a collage of kitchen utensils. Use the strips as a bulletin board border for a unit on food or healthy eating habits.

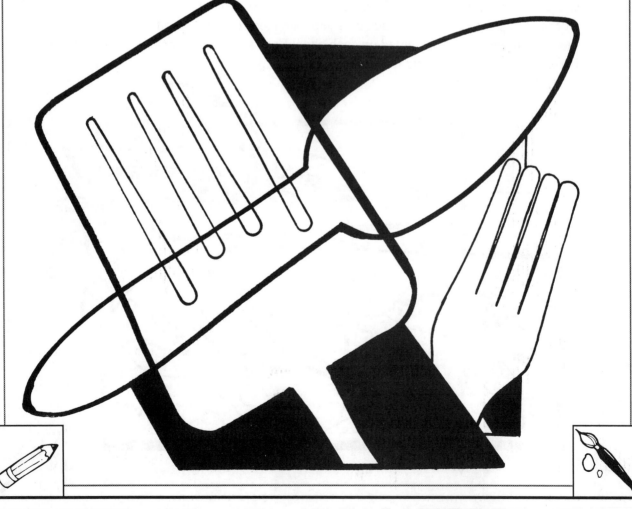

Cellophane Butterflies

Materials

black construction paper; scissors; colored cellophane; glue or stapler

Directions

1. Place one piece of black construction paper on top of another and draw an outline of a butterfly. (For younger children, you may want to make a stencil first.)

2. Cut out the inside of each wing section, as shown.

3. Cut cellophane paper to cover the outline of the butterfly. Glue the cellophane between the two black butterfly outlines.

4. Trim away excess cellophane.

5. To decorate the transparent part of the wings, add small pieces of construction paper or sequins to the cellophane.

Extensions

- Decorate windows or make a wall display to celebrate spring.
- Hang butterflies from the ceiling.
- Use cellophane butterflies for a science display or center or for a poetry unit on insects.

Tissue Paper Flowers

Materials

one 9" x 12" (23 cm x 30 cm) sheet of white construction paper for each student; green watercolors or markers; glue; scissors; pencil; colored tissue paper

Directions

1. On the white construction paper, draw an outline of a few flowers complete with stems and leaves. Leave a 1" (2.54 cm) border around the paper.

2. With green watercolors or markers, color stems and leaves.

3. Cut colored tissue paper into circles about the size of a half dollar. The circles will serve as petals for each flower. Make five or six circles for each flower.

4. To form a petal, evenly cover the end of a pencil with a circle, and pull up around the pencil. Dip the tissue circle at the pencil end lightly in glue and place the petal on the flower drawing. Continue making and gluing petals until all petals are covered.

5. Make the 3-D frame by folding in the construction paper about 1" (2.54 cm) along the edges. Tape, staple, or glue the corners together.

Extensions

• Make flowers using the petal-making process described above and attach them to border displays and bulletin boards with spring themes.

Popcorn Trees

Materials

black construction paper; any other color construction paper; scissors; glue; popped popcorn

Directions

1. Using black construction paper, have students trace around each other's arms to form trees. (White pencil or chalk works well for tracing.)

2. Cut out a tree pattern. Glue the tree on any color construction paper.

3. Glue popcorn to the tree. (Use colored popcorn if available.)

4. Treat students to the remaining popcorn!

Extensions

- Replace paper trees with twigs or small branches.
- Write popcorn poems or tell the "Story of Popcorn" on index cards and display them along with the popcorn trees.

Paper Bag Puppets

Materials

paper lunch/sandwich bags; markers, crayons, or paints; scissors; glue

Directions

1. Make a face and other body parts for the puppet character. Be sure the parts are in proportion to the size of the bag. The face should be as large as, or a little larger than the bottom of the bag; the torso should fit on the front or back of the bag.

2. Cut out and decorate the puppet pieces.

3. Turn the bag upside down so that the bottom of the bag faces up. Do not open the bag. Glue the head piece on the bottom flap.

4. Glue the torso of the puppet onto the flat, rectangular part of the bag just below the lower part of the head piece.

5. If the puppet has separate arms, glue them to the left and right of the character on the narrow, rectangular sides of the bag.

6. Place your hand inside the bag to make the puppet talk and move.

Extensions

• Create new characters or make characters based on familiar stories or fairy tales. Make a puppet show stage using a large carton. Prepare puppet shows using the paper bag puppets. Two Paper Bag puppet patterns are provided on pages 88-89.

Stuffed Bag Characters

Materials

white or brown paper lunch bags (You will need three bags per character.); newspaper; string; markers, crayons, or paints; scissors; glue

Directions

1. Tear newspaper into strips. The strips are used for stuffing the bag.

2. Stuff one of the bags with newspaper.

3. Lay a paper bag flat on a surface with the opening at the bottom. Draw the body of the character on the side facing up.

4. Slide the bag with the body sketch over the stuffed bag. Glue the bags together or tie them together at the middle with string.

5. Turn another closed bag upside down and draw a face. Leave about three inches (8 cm) of room at the opening to tie the bag. Stuff the bag with newspaper and tie it with string.

6. Glue or tape the head onto the body.

7. If desired, add arms and legs. (For accordion-folded arms and legs, see page 23.)

Extensions

- Make stuffed bag characters to represent fictional characters from books the students are reading.

- Use stuffed bag characters for holiday or special occasion displays.

- Have students make stuffed bag characters of themselves. Use the characters as part of a representation of each student's written work, projects, etc.

Treasure Boxes

Materials

a variety of uncooked pastas; Colorful Pasta recipe (page 86); glue; cigar boxes or shoe boxes (with tops)

Directions

1. Gather a variety of pastas—shells, elbow macaroni, bowties, etc. Store each type in its own container.

2. Color pasta using the directions on page 86.

3. Have students glue pasta on the sides and top of the shoe box or cigar box. (To create an attached top for a shoe box, slit the corners on one side of the top and glue the separated edge to the shoe box.) Fill the entire surface with pasta, or cover only the top with pasta and the sides with wallpaper, fabric, or construction paper.

Extensions

• Use the decorated boxes as gifts or to store special items, notes, materials, etc.

• If the class is divided into groups or tables, have each group of students make a treasure box for its table. Store important materials for the group in the treasure boxes.

String Art

Materials

string or yarn; construction paper; hole punch; markers

Directions

1. Have students print their first names in capital letters across the top of a piece of construction paper near the edge.

2. Punch a hole below each letter.

3. Next, ask students to print their last names in capital letters across the bottom of the paper near the edge. Punch a hole above each letter.

4. Attach string or yarn from the holes at the top of the paper to holes at the bottom as illustrated below. Thread a length of yarn or string back and forth through the holes by beginning at the top left corner and finishing at the bottom left corner. (Be sure to make a knot in the back of the first hole to secure the yarn.)

5. If students' first and last names do not have the same number of letters, have them add stars, hearts, or a small illustration of their own on either end of the shorter name so that the number of letters on the top and bottom of the paper will match.

Extensions

- Make string art pictures for matching facts or for problem-solving activities.
- Collect rectangular pieces of thin cardboard such as sketch pad or writing pad backings. Punch one or two rows of holes along the border of the cardboard and weave colorful yarn or string through the holes to create a frame. Students can use these to frame pictures, stories, poems, etc.

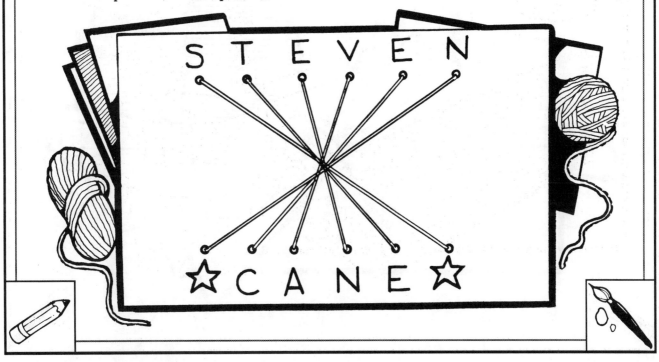

Napkin Art

Materials

paper napkins or paper towels; food coloring; water; bowls; newspaper

Directions

1. Cover the work surface with newspaper.

2. Prepare bowls of different food colorings by adding a small amount of water and a few drops of food coloring to each bowl. Students will enjoy mixing colors, such as red and blue to make purple.

3. Fold the napkin/paper towel in half, then in half again. Keep folding until it is small.

4. Dip each corner of the napkin/paper towel in food coloring.

5. Unfold the napkin/paper towel and allow it to dry on the newspaper.

Extensions

- Make "gift-giver" napkins. Fold the napkin back into its original shape. (Fold the paper towel in half, then in half again.) Accordion-fold the napkin/paper towel and pinch it in the middle. Tie a piece of yarn or ribbon in the center. Spread the ends out to create a fan shape on each side. Slip a small gift through the yarn at the center of the napkin. Gift suggestions: a new pencil; a candy cane or lollipop; a poem, gift certificate, special coupon, or award rolled up like a scroll.

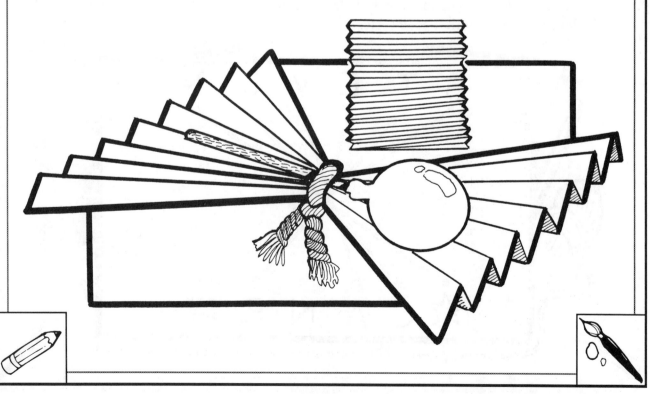

72

Tissue Paper Collages

Materials

a variety of colored art tissue paper; brushes of various widths; containers of thinned white glue or laundry starch; scissors; pencils or markers for sketches; white or light-colored construction paper for background; newspaper

Directions

1. Cover the work area with newspaper.

2. Begin by tearing a few small pieces of tissue of different colors and overlapping them on a small piece of white construction paper. (For best results, place dark colors on top of light colors.)

3. Brush the top surface with starch. The liquid penetrates the thin paper, blends the colors, and bonds the tissue to the background sheet.

   Hints: The brush may pick up color from the tissue and spread it to the background paper. This can become part of the design or can be avoided by stopping the brush before it reaches the background paper. Subtle shadings can be obtained by overlapping pieces of the same tissue color. Brilliant combinations and contrasts appear when different colors overlap.

4. Let the tissue dry thoroughly before adding details and textures. Add subject matter by sketching an outline or make planned shapes without one. Fill in the outline with tissue. (Tissue can be cut to a sharp edge, torn for a softer look, or added in small pieces to fill in an outline.)

Extensions

- Fill in the outlines and/or shapes using paint applied with brushes, sponges, or a variety of fabrics and objects. Or, print the paint on with spools, bottle caps, plastic forks, or vegetables.

Attention Getters

Materials

paper plates; craft sticks or tongue depressors; scissors; glue; markers, crayons, or paint; materials for decorating plates

Directions

1. Cut paper plates in half.

2. Glue a craft stick or tongue depressor in the middle of the straight edge of the plate so that two-thirds of the stick projects out from the straight edge.

3. Label the paper plate sign with an appropriate name for a center, group, table, activity, etc. Or, decorate the plate to represent a special holiday or project.

Extensions

• Use the paper plate signs and decorations to call attention to a center, an area of the room, or a group activity in which a nonverbal response is required.

• Make streamers from construction paper, art tissue, or newspaper and glue them to the curved portion of the plate. Use the "attention getters" for celebrations or parades.

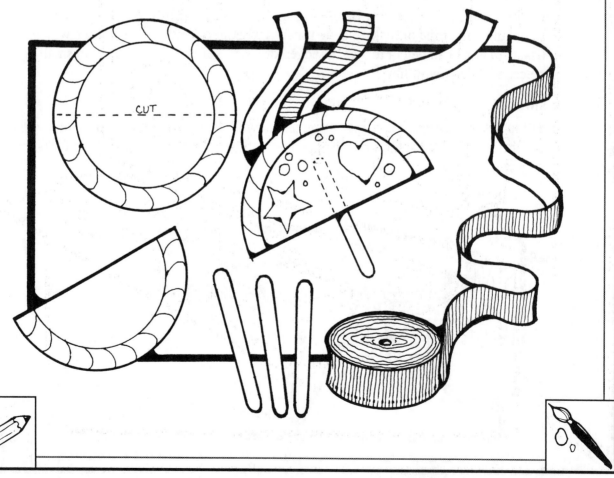

Story Boxes

Materials

shoe boxes; scraps from paper products, objects from nature, material remnants, small boxes, buttons, shells, etc.; glue or tape; paint, crayons, or markers; scissors

Directions

• Using any kind of project materials stored in the classroom, or scraps brought from home, have students create scenes inside the shoe boxes.

Extensions

• Make scenes from books, historical events, or nature.

• Attach story boxes to bulletin boards for a three-dimensional effect.

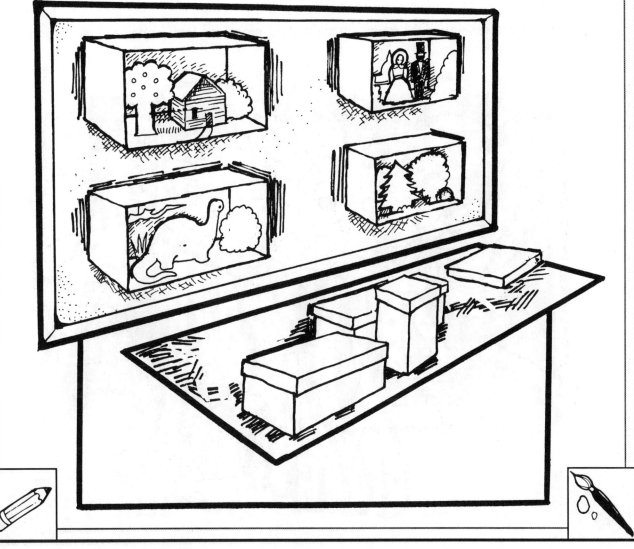

Creatures

Materials

newspapers; string or yarn; scrap materials; computer paper tear-off edges; glue; scissors; crayons, markers, or paints

Directions

1. Roll up a sheet of newspaper to form a creature body.

2. Tie each end with string or yarn.

3. Using scrap materials, glue eyes, ears, mouth, and nose to the center of the newspaper body.

4. Make tentacles by gluing computer paper edges to the creature.

5. Color as desired.

6. Write a story about your creature and share it with others.

Extensions

- Hang creatures around the room. Attach riddles, problems, interesting or unusual facts, poems, etc., to them.

"Dot" Poems

Materials

construction paper; hole punch; glue

Directions

1. Punch holes in a variety of colors of construction paper. Collect the hole punch "dots."

2. When you have enough, give each student an envelope of colorful "dots." Ask students to glue dotted frames around illustrated stories they have written. Display the framed stories.

Extensions

- Use the hole punch "dots" as a filler for other art media.

- Make mosaic-like pictures from the "dots" and write stories or poems about the pictures.

- Have students use dots to form the letters of their first names. Glue the dot letters vertically on a piece of paper. Ask students to write poems or acrostics using the letters of their names.

- Ask students to form a series of numbers, as in a zip code or phone number, using the hole punch "dots." Glue the numbers vertically on a piece of paper. Write related poems in which the number of words or syllables on a line matches the dotted number.

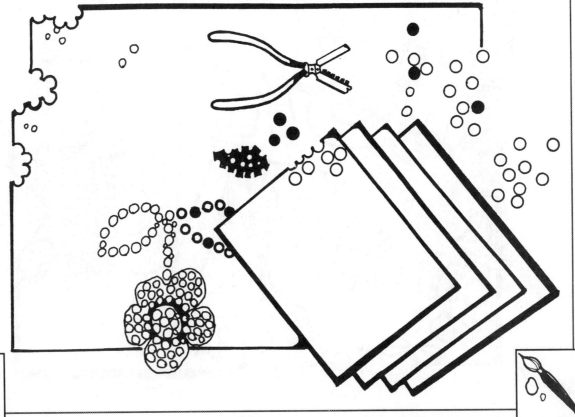

What's in a Name?

Materials

construction paper or index paper; glue; markers; raw beans, rice, corn, or sunflower seeds

Directions

1. On white construction paper or index paper, have students use markers to outline their first names. Make large upper-case letters. Younger children may need to have an older partner or adult assist with the letters. Letter stencils are provided on pages 92-94.

2. Put glue inside the outline of the first letter and add beans, rice, corn, or seeds to fill in the letter.

3. Continue adding glue and beans, rice, corn, or seeds until all the letters are covered.

4. Allow the glue to dry overnight.

5. Have students cut around their names. Glue the name to another color construction paper.

Extensions

- Glue the "dots" made from the punched-out holes of colorful construction paper inside the outline of the letters. Or, use thick yarn or twine around the outline. Next, have students fill the inside of the letters with poems or phrases that describe themselves. Allow each student to use the finished product as a cover for a journal.

78

Hanger People Self-Portraits

Materials

hangers; long-sleeved old shirts (one per student); white paper plates; stapler; scissors; markers or crayons; red, yellow, brown, and black yarn (for hair); construction paper

Directions

1. Have students draw their faces on the bottom of a paper plate. Add hair by gluing yarn to the plate.

2. Place the plate over the hook portion of the hanger.

3. Place a second plate face-up under the hanger, lining it up with the top plate.

4. Attach the two plates, with the center of the hanger in between them, by stapling together the perimeters of the plates.

5. Hang the shirt on the hanger.

6. Make hands from construction paper and staple them to the sleeves.

Extensions

• Use the self-portraits to feature a "Student of the Week/Month."

• Place the students' hanger people at their desks for Open House. Display student work on the desks. Have students write notes to their visiting families and pin them to the shirts of the hanger people.

Ghost Stories

Materials

cardboard; newspaper; white paper; scissors; glue; markers; stapler

Directions

1. Cover a rectangular piece of cardboard (any size) with newspaper.

2. Using white paper, draw and cut out a large ghost.

3. Glue the ghost in the middle of the newspaper-covered cardboard.

4. Have students write scary stories.

5. Glue each story to the bottom half of the cardboard.

Extensions

- Make a 3-D ghost to attach to the cardboard. Wad up newspaper for a head and use white cloth to cover the head and form the body. Tie the cloth with white string around the neck, allowing the remaining cloth to drape. Use markers to draw eyes and a mouth on the head of the ghost. Glue or staple the ghost to the cardboard. Add scary stories or poems.

Triptych Frames

Materials

cardboard; scissors; ruler; crayons, paint, or markers; wallpaper scraps; glue

Directions

1. Measure and cut a rectangular piece of cardboard. (One 12" x 24"/ 30 cm x 60 cm piece per project works well.)

2. Place the cardboard on a work surface. Measure the length of the cardboard and divide it into thirds. Mark the divisions and draw a line to show the thirds.

3. Complete frames by cutting wallpaper into thin strips and gluing the strips all around the edge of the cardboard and along the division lines. (This will make three framed sections.)

4. Have students write poems to fit inside the middle section of their triptych frames. Next, illustrate the poems and glue the illustrations inside the last section of the triptych frame. Use the first section for a poem title or a photo of the poem's author.

Extensions

• Make triptych frames as gifts. Reproduce a famous poem or quote that reflects the qualities of the person who will receive the gift. Glue it in the center section. Write the recipient's name in the first section. Include a personal greeting in the last section.

Honeycomb Heart Cards

Materials

honeycomb pads (available at some teacher supply stores and art supply stores); 9" x 12" (23 cm x 30 cm) pieces of pink construction paper or index paper; red construction paper; glue; scissors; markers, crayons, or colored pencils

Directions

1. Fold a piece of pink construction paper in half.

2. Use red construction paper to design and cut out a valentine for the front cover of the card. Glue the valentine to the cover and add a valentine greeting.

3. Have students open the card to the inside. Cut a square of honeycomb paper. (Be sure to cut an appropriately sized piece to fit in the center of the inside of the card.) Draw an outline of half of a heart along the edge of the honeycomb square. Cut out the pattern.

4. Apply glue to the back and front of the heart half. To glue the heart in the center, place the straight edge of the heart against the fold and close the card. Allow the glue to dry.

5. Write a valentine message on the inside.

Extensions

• Add yarn, ribbon, or confetti made from cut pieces of construction paper to the inside or cover of the card.

• Make cards for other occasions. Match the honeycomb patterns to the occasion.

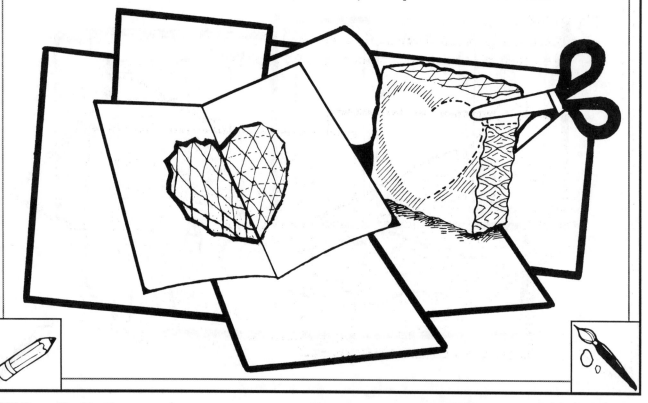

Sponge Print Haiku

Materials

sponges; tempera paints; scissors; construction paper; markers; foil or styrofoam trays; soap, water, and towels for clean-up; newspaper; glue

Directions

1. Take a nature walk with the class and observe the elements of nature. Have students use their observations to write haiku poetry. Haiku is poetry of seventeen syllables arranged in three lines of 5-7-5 syllables. It may contain direct or indirect references to the seasons or to nature.

2. Prepare sponge print backgrounds. On a sponge, have each student use a marker to outline the object (tree, fish, cloud, etc.) he or she chose to write about in the Haiku poem. Cut out the object.

3. Cover work area with newspaper.

4. Pour tempera paint in trays and distribute construction paper.

5. Create sponge prints by pressing sponges into the paint and stamping the print onto the construction paper. Fill the paper with prints that reflect the subject of the haiku poem. Allow the paint to dry.

6. Have students glue their haiku poems to the sponge print backgrounds.

   Note: Younger children can make the sponge print backgrounds and dictate information about an object of nature to an older partner or an adult.

Extensions

• Make sponge prints of items for holidays and other special occasions. Use prints to decorate cards, bulletin boards, or frames for displays.

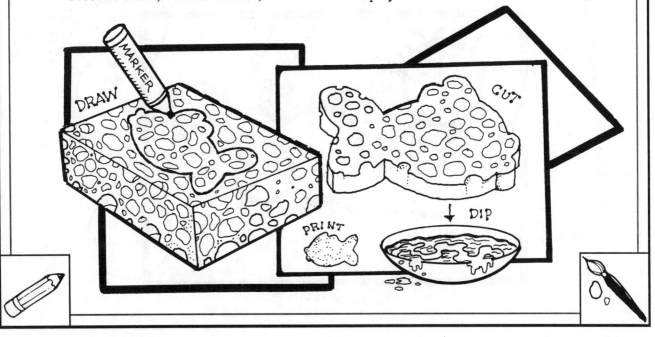

Bubble-Splash Collages

Send home a Messy Day Reminder ahead of time. (See page 96.)

Make arrangements to do this activity outside in an open area.

Materials

various colors of tempera paint; $\frac{1}{4}$ cup (50 mL) measuring cup; $\frac{1}{2}$ gallon (about 2 L) bubble solution; 6"-12" (15 cm-30 cm) bubble wands (see page 87 for directions); white construction paper; large plastic container (with lid); large plastic trash bags

Directions

1. Prepare bubble solution using directions on page 87.

   Mix $\frac{1}{4}$ cup of desired color paint into bubble solution. (Add more for a darker color.)

2. Place the bubble solution container on a large plastic trash bag. Blow colored bubbles in the air and have students try to catch the bubbles on their papers.

3. When the bubbles break on the paper, they leave a spectacular array of colored splotches. After students have created their bubble splash art, set the papers in an area to dry.

4. On a wall or large bulletin board, arrange the individual papers in a collage.

Extensions

- Have students write about their bubble experience or create poems or stories about bubbles. Display these on the bubble-splash collage.

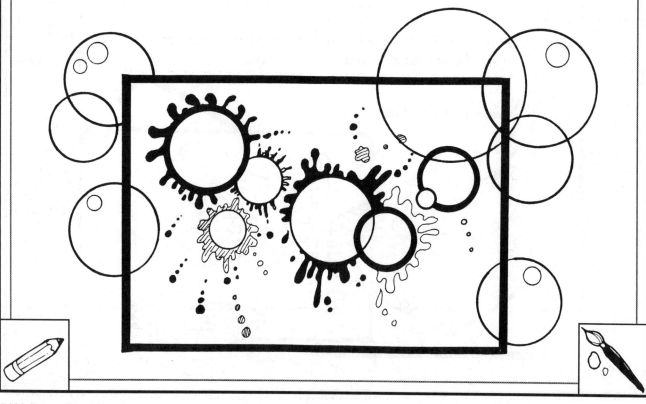

Supply Request Letter

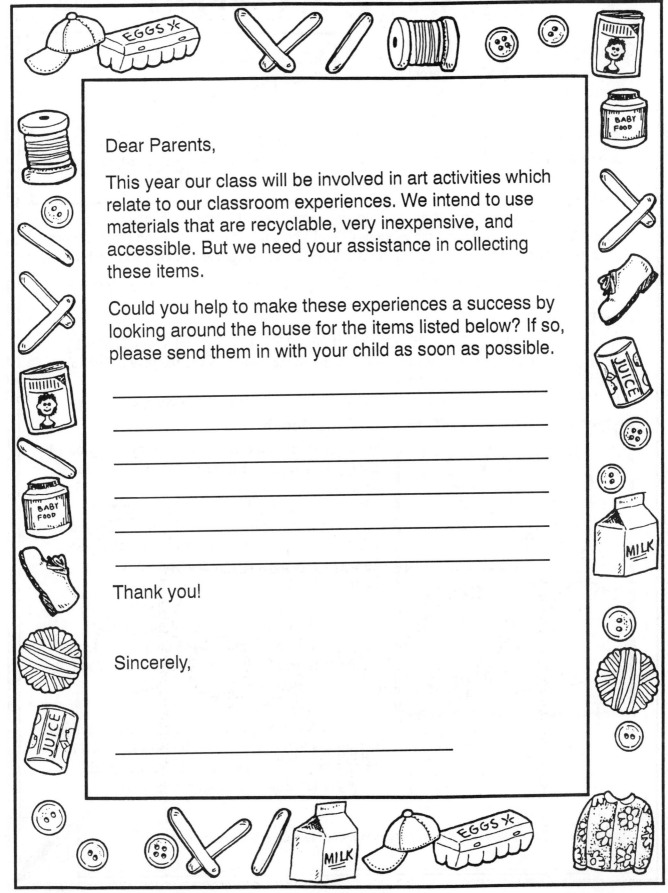

Dear Parents,

This year our class will be involved in art activities which relate to our classroom experiences. We intend to use materials that are recyclable, very inexpensive, and accessible. But we need your assistance in collecting these items.

Could you help to make these experiences a success by looking around the house for the items listed below? If so, please send them in with your child as soon as possible.

_____

_____

_____

_____

_____

Thank you!

Sincerely,

_____

Homemade Art Supplies

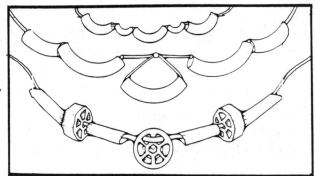

Colorful Pasta

Prepare various colors of macaroni for projects ahead of time by soaking uncooked macaroni in food coloring diluted with water. (Adding a little rubbing alcohol helps the macaroni dry more quickly.)

Watercolors

Make your own watercolors using the following ingredients: 1 teaspoon (5 mL) water; 1 tablespoon (15 mL) vinegar; 2 tablespoons (30 mL) baking soda; 1 tablespoon (15 mL) corn starch; $1/2$ teaspoon (2.5 mL) glycerin; food coloring. Mix vinegar and baking soda in a small cup or bowl. Add remaining ingredients and stir.

Play Dough

In a mixing bowl, knead 1 cup (250 mL) salt, 1 cup (250 mL) flour, and $1/2$ cup (125 mL) water. If desired, add a few drops of food coloring to the dough. Store the play dough in a sealable plastic container or plastic bag.

Inedible Dough

In a large saucepan, combine 1 cup (250 mL) flour, 1 cup (250 mL) water, 1 tablespoon (15 mL) salad oil, 2 teaspoons (10 mL) cream of tartar, $1/2$ cup (125 mL) salt, and desired food coloring. Stir the mixture constantly over medium heat, using a wooden spoon. When the dough begins to stick together enough to form a ball, remove it from the heat source, but continue stirring.

Place the hot ball of dough on a floured surface. Knead the dough as it cools. The dough will be soft and pliable for molding into whatever shapes are needed for an art project.

You can make the dough in advance of an art activity and store it in the refrigerator. It also keeps well in a covered container in the freezer. Use the dough recipe for art projects throughout the year.

Homemade Art Supplies *(cont.)*

Bubble Solution

In a large container with lid, mix 1 gallon (about 4 L) of water, 1 cup (250 mL) liquid dish detergent, and 40-60 drops of glycerine. Stir well. Cover the container. Let the solution stand for about one week. (Aging the bubble solution allows it to produce thicker soap films.)

Bubble Wand

To make a bubble wand you will need a hanger, three feet (1 meter) of cotton string, pliers, scissors, electrical or duct tape. Prepare the bubble solution using the directions on this page. Bend the middle section of the wire hanger into a desired shape. Twist the end sections together to form a handle. To avoid sharp edges, cover the handle with tape.

Note to the teacher: Create very large bubbles with two plastic drinking straws and four foot (1.2 m) length of string. Pull the string through the straws and knot the ends. Place the bubble maker in the solution. As you gently lift the bubble maker out, spread the straws out the form a rectangular shape. Pass the bubble maker through the air to create huge bubbles.

Homemade Ink

This process is similar to one of the first ways writing ink was produced. The homemade ink can be used for writing activities and art projects. Homemade ink can be made from ripe blueberries or strawberries. Gather the following materials: small jars with lids (Baby food jars work well.), a teaspoon or eye dropper, paper towels, paper cups, and some water.

Remove the stems and leaves from ripe berries. Place the berries in a small jar. Mixing different kinds of berries will produce different colored inks. Press the berries to a pulp with the back of a spoon. When the berries are crushed, add water, one drop at a time, using a teaspoon or eye dropper. (The more water you add the lighter the color the ink will be.) Stir the mixture well.

Place a sheet of paper towel over a paper cup. Push the paper towel down into the cup. Slowly pour the berry mixture through the towel pressed into the cup. Let all of the liquid drain through the towel. This is the slow part of the process. Remove the towel and throw it away. Pour the strained ink back into the jar. Use the jar as an ink container. The homemade ink can be used to write letters, poems, and stories. Or, dip a paintbrush in the ink and use it for a painting project.

Paper Bag Puppet Patterns

Follow directions for making puppets on page 68.

Paper Bag Puppet Patterns *(cont.)*

Follow directions for making puppets on page 68.

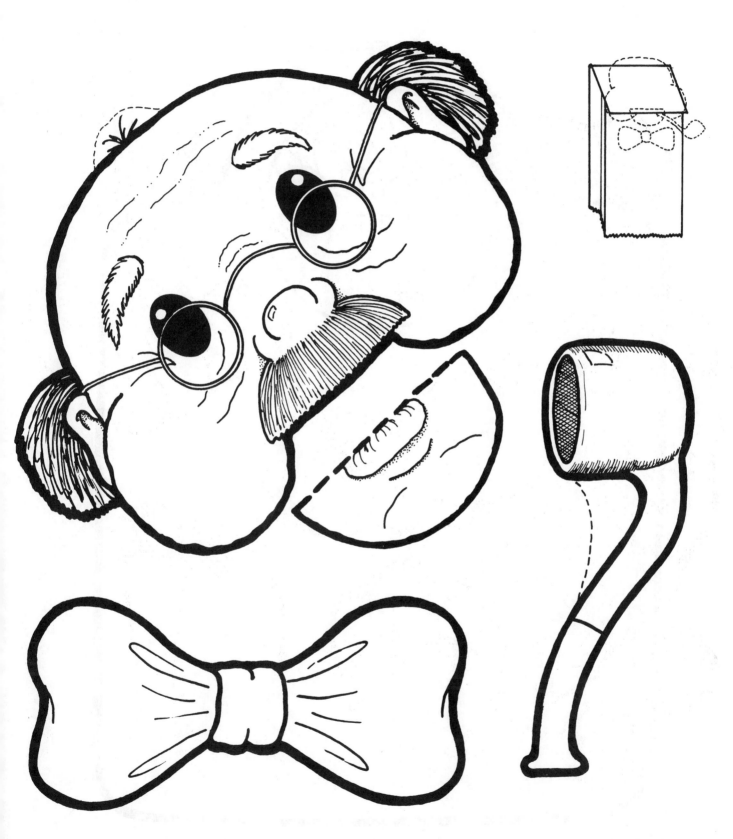

Door Knob Hanger Pattern

Directions: Reproduce the pattern below onto construction paper or tagboard. Cut out. Decorate the door knob hanger using crayons, markers, paper scraps, etc. Cut out the marked circle and along the dashed line. Hang on a door knob.

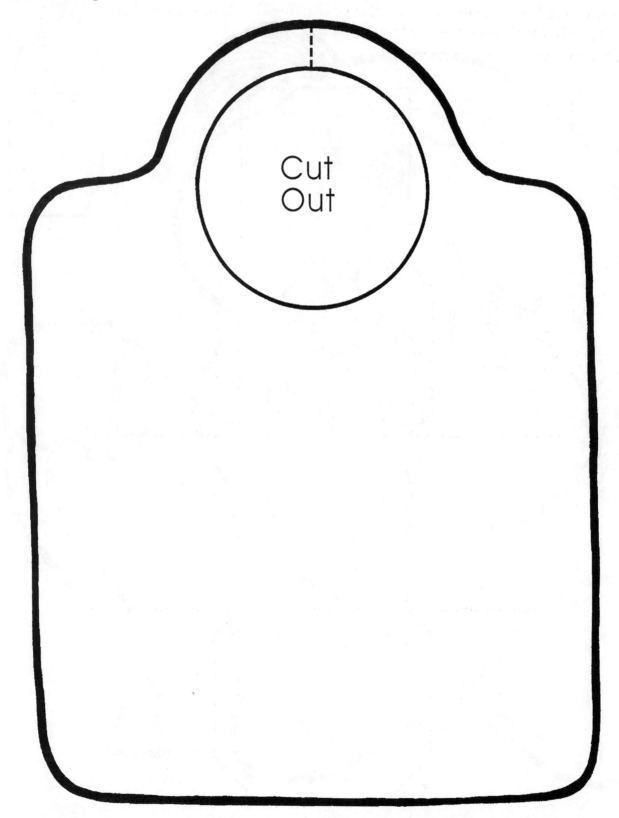

Cut Out

Box Pattern

Directions: Reproduce the pattern below on index paper or construction paper. Cut out the pattern along the solid lines. Fold along the dotted lines and glue the tabs in place to form the box. Allow glue to dry.

Have students decorate the box with designs, written messages, or theme-related illustrations. Tape string or yarn to one side of the box and hang it for display.

Note: You may wish to enlarge the pattern.

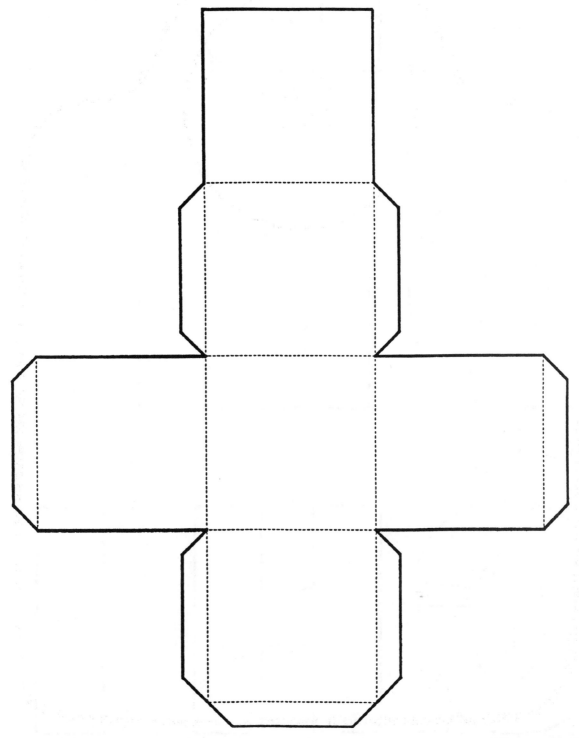

Letters

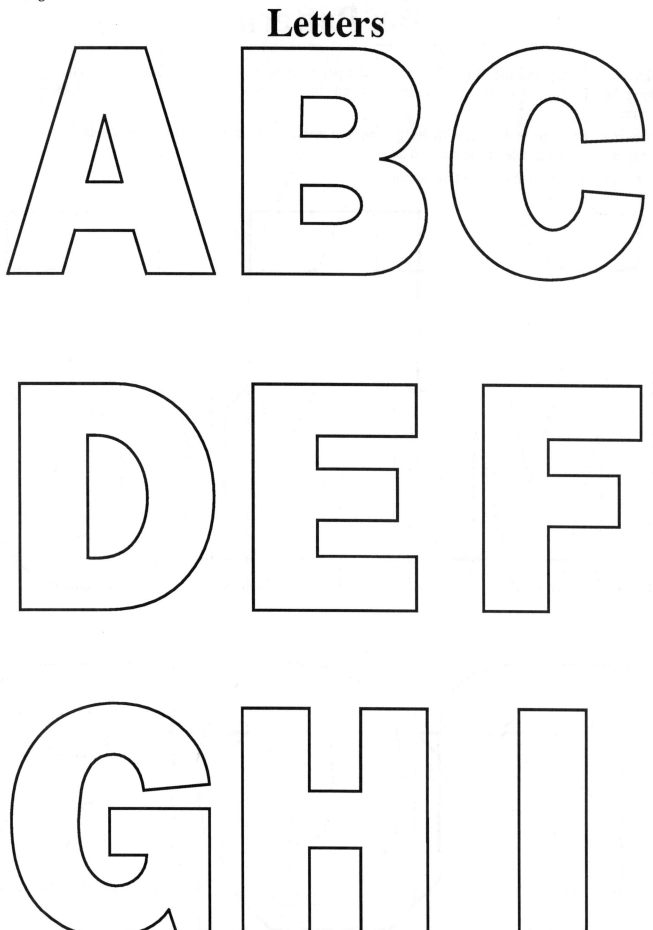

Letters *(cont.)*

Letters *(cont.)*

Numbers

Messy Day Reminders

Use these reminders to inform parents and children of upcoming art activities that may become a bit messy.

We need to dress for mess

on _____ ,
(Date)

when we will be

_____ .
(Activity)

_____
Student's Signature

A messy day is

coming our way

on _____ ,
(Date)

when we will be

_____ .
(Activity)

_____
Student's Signature

96